The Manly Pursuit of Desire and Love

Your Guide to Life, Happiness, and Emotional and Sexual Fulfillment In a Closed-Down World

Perry Brass

by the author of *The Manly Art of Seduction, The Substance of God, How to Survive Your Own Gay Life,* and *King of Angels*

Belhue Press

Belhue Press, First Edition, First Printing

Copyright 2015 © Perry Brass

Published in the United States of America by:

Belhue Press
2501 Palisade Avenue, Suite A1
Bronx, NY 10463

Electronic mail address: belhuepress@earthlink.net

Cover and inside book design by Tom Saettel
Cover painting by George Towne
Andy Seated, 2009, Oil on canvas, 28 x 22 in.
For more about George Towne, please see page 220

ISBN (10): 1-892149-20-6
ISBN: (13): 978-1-892149-20-6

Library of Congress Control Number: 2015933066

BISAC category code: SEL034000 (SELF-HELP / Sexual Instruction)

SEL016000 (SELF-HELP / Personal Growth / Happiness)

Publisher's Cataloging-in-Publication

    Brass, Perry.
       The Manly pursuit of desire and love : your guide to life , happiness , and emotional and sexual fulfillment in a closed-down world / Perry Brass.
       p. cm.
       ISBN 978-1-892149-20-6

       1. Men --Sexual behavior. 2. Sex (Psychology). 3. Sexual health. 4. Male homosexuality. 5. Identity (Psychology). 6. Sex behavior. 7. Desire. 8. Masculinity. I. Title.

       HQ76 .B79 2015
       306.76/62 --dc23   2015933066

ACKNOWLEDGEMENTS AND THANKS

I really need to thank many people for making this book possible. First, my husband Hugh Young, and my friend Ricardo Limon without whose help I could not have written this. Also Ron Suresha, Tom Saettel, and my friend Jim Marks; the staff of the Leslie-Lohman Museum of Gay and Lesbian Art, specifically, Hunter O'Hanian, Jerry Kajpust, and Branden Charles Wallace; and the generosity of George Towne, and also my friends who encouraged this book, and helped me to continue with it even in those moments when I lost heart.

Other Books by Perry Brass

Sex-charge (poetry)

Mirage, a science fiction novel

Works and Other 'Smoky George' Stories

Circles, the sequel to Mirage

Out There: Stories of Private Desires. Horror.
And the Afterlife

Albert or The Book of Man,
the third book in the Mirage series

Works and Other 'Smoky George' Stories,
Expanded Edition

The Harvest, a "science/politico" novel

The Lover of My Soul, A Search for Ecstasy
and Wisdom (poetry and other collected writings)

How to Survive Your <u>Own</u> Gay Life,
An Adult Guide to Love, Sex, and Relationships

Angel Lust, An Erotic Novel of Time Travel

Warlock, A Novel of Possession

The Substance of God, A Spiritual Thriller

The Manly Art of Seduction, How to Meet, Talk to, and
Become Intimate with Anyone

King of Angels, A Novel About the Genesis of Identity
and Belief

Carnal Sacraments, A Historical Novel of the Future,
Set in the Last Quarter of the 21st Century, 2nd Edition

CONTENTS

Part One
The Foundation:
Approaching, Supporting,
and Expanding
Your Own Desires

1 The Manly Pursuit of Desire and You

If you are what you eat, then why aren't you what you desire?

Desire stands in the great no man's land of human activity: the zone of most conflict, fear, and anxiety. It scares us. We are often asked to hate it—by those who claim to have given it up for "better" things, and who often, hypocritically, haven't. Their biggest desire is power, and *desire*, whether you are for it or against it, is a blast furnace of power. Your own desires are an opening to the tightly held world of your imagination, your real feelings, and your Self. The larger Deeper Self, the Self that contains that core of your own regeneration we call the "soul." That is, the part of you that you want—against all rationalism—to survive death. The part that is strong, tender, and closest to that revelation of your own creation, either in a biological sense, or within the process of our own "self-creation"—the process of coming into ourselves—which we all seek.

Desire, then, is right *there*. It is inside that mysterious cocoon within us containing the very soul of us. It cannot be divided from that amazing package we call *us*.

This may be a hard thing for many people to get their heads around, but I will speak about it many times in this book.

But first, let's get this settled:

I have no p.c. agenda in this book, and there may be some things here that will raise the hairs on the back of your neck. Basically I want to explore what makes us *us*: our most basic desires and the feelings under them, and the even deeper longings under those feelings. Our sexual desires, of course, and also our personal, psychological, and even spiritual ones. They are all intertwined, and waiting. Therefore, if you have that most basic desire of all—*curiosity*—as well as a hunger for self-knowledge and a need to question your own inhibitions and fears, please keep reading.

Note: I wrote this book because I felt that, after writing *The Manly Art of Seduction*, many people were still missing out on the very *positive* joys of seduction because they were afraid of their own basic selves within their deepest desires. *The Manly Art of Seduction* is still very popular, but I've talked to enough men and women who told me that there was, even still, another aspect of themselves missing. They didn't understand this aspect. It inhibited them very much. And it wasn't just fear of rejection, even as strong as that fear is.

Finally, I started to understand what this aspect was. They could not make peace with their own desires, their own secret personal places. So I started the adventure of writing this book for them, and for you. I hope you will join me in this exploration of desire, and I have places in this book, as I did in *The Manly Art of Seduction*, for your own participation and input, because without that, *The Manly Pursuit of Desire and Love* would only be a one-sided venture, and I want you to be a part of this, too.

CHAPTER 2

18 Things You Need to Know About Desire Before You Read This Book

"They say I am queer, prince, but I can tell what people are like. For the heart is the great thing, and the rest is nonsense."

The Idiot, Fyodor Dostoevsky.

1. Desire is deeper than simple horniness, want, and hunger. Desire is you asking for completion, identity, and enlargement. It is a large component of consciousness.

2. It is a key to the deepest parts of yourself. The parts we often label your "soul," or your "spiritual" feelings, or the basic aspects of your own ego and character. I will refer often in this book to the "Deeper Self," that is, that engine of your own deepest imagination working through experiences, where the keys to all of your feelings, personality, and drives lie. I will talk about the Deeper Self, how to connect with it and use that connection to bond with other people. How to experience huge joy and happiness from this connection, and expand with it.

3. Destroying and/or obstructing desire can lead to depression.

4. Desire has many facets, branches, and streams to it, often illuminating deeper parts of your experiences and personality, which you have either forgotten or have chosen to deny.

5. Being able to share desire with another person is what leads to genuine intimacy.

6. Understanding how desire works (and how it is repressed), allows you to understand much of the nature of yourself, as well as society's own nature.

7. The spiritual aspects of desire are often repressed because they are so powerful. Many people who cannot deal honestly with these aspects often find extreme *shame* in them.

8. Desire is a part of consciousness, and yet runs deeper than consciousness.

9. The boundaries we put around desire very much constitute our own images of ourselves. Changing these boundaries (as well as seeing the boundaries for what they are) can be very important to you, and can become part of your own life changes.

10. A lot of what we call "therapy" is about either reinforcing these boundaries, or acknowledging them without actually opening them up to your own Deeper Self: that most basic inner part of you.

11. Love is more than physical desire but is a part of a greater desire that exists within your Deeper Self.

12. All of consciousness is understanding desire, not simply rejecting it.

13. Much of what we call "art" is about expressing desire.

14. Understanding desire and its place in your life can break harmful cycles of loneliness, depression, guilt, and shame.

15. The deepest love and feeling is allowing someone into your own "field of desire."

16. This field of desire brings you back to a state of both vast consciousness and the genuine blissful innocence that many if not most of us seek through religion.

17. Desire as a sensual and psychological expression of your Deeper Self can be extended to reach into all parts of your life, and make you very happy.

18. Shame, guilt, self-consciousness, and self-abnegation, enforced on us by parental and social taboos, repressive religion, job requirements, or other aspects of society, systematically destroy our ability to understand the power of desire and how it fits into our real lives.

3 One Basic Question About Your Own Happiness

If you are not happy, what's keeping you from being happy? I know, you've asked yourself this, unless your friends (the honest ones at least) have been asking it for you.

Here is a rundown of answers to that question, and I hope by the end of this book, you will have found ways to deal with all of them.

Isolation—from others, and most important from your own Deeper Self. You'll learn more about this Deeper Self in the next chapter, but keep on reading.

Fear—of being hurt, rejected, or humiliated.

Fear—of your deepest desires and the feelings under them, and not knowing how to express these desires safely, and how to satisfy them.

Fear—of the real person inside you, from whom you've been hiding for so many years.

Fear—of actually being alive, because you've been taught for so long of the "price" you'll be forced to pay.

"Reality"—that scariest of all things, certainly as defined by other people who frankly love to define it for you. And your embrace of this "reality" at the same time as it has been destroying you. Here I am talking about social "realities," family "realities," job and business "realities," economic "realities," and of course religious and "moral" "realities."

Now it's time to start the rest of the book, but if you have another answer to this important personal question, please write it here.

_____

_____

_____

4

15 Desires and You, & Fast Track Desires

"Desire is the essence of a man."

Baruch Spinoza

Here we have fifteen basic desires that I feel lie at the root of most of our drives, fantasies, and wishes. Many of you will have an "Ah-ha!" moment with these, and some of you will find them a discovery waiting for you to happen upon. But the important thing is for you to realize how universal they are.

You will find that in this list I bring up the important concept of the "Deeper Self." This is that part of you that remains with you all your life; I will talk about it often and seriously in the rest of this book.

1. The desire to recover or assume [re-gather] innocence, and in doing so experience love. The desire to return to childhood innocence, to approach its simplicity, beauty, sweetness, and gentleness. (Often within this desire is a need to block out the pain, traumas, and ruthlessness of childhood. For many of us, childhood is a time when much pain is inflicted on us, and, for some of us, it is also a period when we've been capable of inflicting pain on others.)

This desire to return to innocence, to become pure, "virginal" inside again, is at the heart of many religious practices that believe that consciousness itself is evil (remember that wily snake in the Garden of Eden?), and that idealizes "pre-consciousness" (i.e., the state of childhood innocence) as ecstatic and pure and which we often believe drives that feeling of love. Therefore sexually, returning to a state of innocence, of even reclaiming virginity, is attractive to many people.

(Unless of course you are still, say, seventeen, and want a nineteen year old to think you're a couple of years older. But even this scenario points to the power of innocence and what a hold it has on us.)

Also, within this first, primary desire to return to innocence is the desire to be disarmed, to lower all defenses and, again, to love and be loved. The desire to love and be loved is a primary feeling behind many of our desires, and it inhabits many of the important personal narratives that I will speak about later.

2. The desire to recover lost, or assume new, power. The desire of all "tops." To be at that place where the force of their own personalities—and the acceptance of it—becomes irresistible, as simply another aspect of nature. In taking on this role, the "top" gets to express his personality, or his idealization of it. However he can also hide the limitations of his own real personality, as the role may be bigger than he is.

In politics, "tops," as less-than-benevolent dictators, get away with murder until they are unmasked as posturing bullies. But in sexual politics, a genuine "top" can find himself expressing a dominant personality he genuinely wants to have, and in doing so *shares* this power with others. This sharing of power is extremely conducive to love, in that it returns us to that innocent, trusting state we desire. This leads us to.

3. The desire to share power and in doing so reveal or display it. Generosity is a source of power, something too often forgotten. One of my main concepts (which I referred to often in *The Manly Art of Seduction*) is the importance of "unbidden" gifts—ones you don't ask for. That is, someone suddenly and generously displays a part of his or her own deepest feelings to you. In our age of withholding feelings, because of self-consciousness and insecurity, the desire to share is often held suspect: it is not part of our cold, "hip" street culture. But there can also be a revelation of true innocence in this sharing—no matter how it's expressed. You are *both* returning to a pristine and emotionally disarmed place where both of you can open up and release deep inner feelings.

In fact, what you are releasing is the beautifully revealed Deeper Self.

4. The desire to reveal vulnerability. (Hopefully safely.) This is often the role of the "bottom," and in doing so it provides an open path or invitation to the innocence within vulnerability. It is also charged with extreme examples of trust, something to which those who "play" within the Dominance and Submission world can attest.

5. The desire to know, and in doing so enlarge yourself. This is an often suppressed desire: knowing has become too loaded with anxiety, even in our "Information Age." Knowing in fact has often become associated with evil or guilt. But the desire to know someone, sexually and emotionally, opens us up to a lot of happiness as well as responsibility. A lot of our feelings about marriage are locked into this desire. Therefore our feelings about our own sexuality, and the deeper "romanticism" under it (and I will go into this later), are fully changed by *knowing*. Knowing becomes larger in fact than simply *carnal* desires, even though the need or want to express these sexual feelings can set us on the path to knowing.

6. **The desire to strip away day-to-day consciousness and in doing so—while losing inhibitions—take on an even greater consciousness.** This desire is often embedded in drug use, what Aldous Huxley called "opening the doors to consciousness," but what he really meant was leaving aside ordinary day-to-day thinking, going into the deeper personal consciousness (i.e., the "Deeper Self") many of us seek.

7. **The desire to transcend death through emotional, spiritual, or sexual exploration.** This desire is embedded in much religious practice, and also in much sexual exploration when we strip away our "normalcy" to find a core of feelings that we often suppress in our day-to-day need to survive. One way to arrive at this is through spiritual and/or sexual rituals, bringing us to a state of suspended timelessness.

In the past exploring this desire was often expressed as "ecstasy," or ecstatic experiences—that is, ones where, through physical associations, you deeply connected with others, even those separated from you through death or from the past of your own "tribe" lost through time.

Some of these feelings can be released through an adrenaline rush (sports, obviously, as well as war and sex do this), or by bringing yourself into a state of deep "alpha" consciousness while awake: that is, experiencing a totally-real dream state while still conscious. A quick road to this is often the use of some drugs within a sexual experience—a road I don't recommend, frankly. But a deeper, more satisfying approach to it can be found in massage work, and in the exquisite experience of slowing down and exchanging feelings including love in a more generous, open, inviting way, and in a very deep state of trust within the same sexual experience.

8. **The desire to relinquish power in exchange for knowledge.** Classically, this was described as a "feminizing" desire, to give up brute force for the calming influence of knowledge. But, as we consider "knowledge to be power," this desire can easily double back on itself, and strengthen you with a power of its own.

9. **The desire for security.** This is one of the most basic of all desires: the return to a childlike state, one of being cared for. Of being warm, secure, and treasured for your own self. *It is the desire we most exhibit in our pursuit of love.* Security gives us the power to extend

ourselves, but in what often feels like limited directions. Therefore the desire for security can suddenly, unexplainably "flip" backward, doing a hundred-and-eighty degree turn, leaving us in a very *unexpected* state of anger and aggression that some of us feel is the "price" for love. I will talk about negative desire later. But for right now, the desire for *security* leads us to status and roles—husband, lover, mate—as well as the strength to shield these roles from problems and adversity.

10.The desire for novelty. The opposite of security, the desire for novelty often makes itself known in feelings of frustration and boredom. We want to be re-ignited with freshness, with new territories of the flesh and of feelings to be explored. This desire also works with the repeated desire to fall in love, as each experience of this intense feeling feels fresh and new, giving us an instant charge that is sometimes followed by a crashing let down.

The same push for novelty is also partnered with an all too-common fear of intimacy, which, despite all the negative P.R. around it, may actually be *justified*. That is, there are legitimate grounds for anxiety about being pent-up, stifled, and inhibited: that is the feeling that you are now compromising your real self, squashing it, and making yourself smaller, often in the pursuit of love. Historyless sex, that is, the pursuit of sex with a *stranger* with whom you have no previous acquaintance, *is* exciting because of this desire for novelty. It means that most agendas have not come into play: a huge amount of judgments have been laid aside. You don't care what his taste in music, books, or politics is.

The only thing you know about one another is the instant attraction you have.

It is scary because of the risks involved—risks to health and safety—but exciting because of this very common desire. But, within this desire, is often a rejection of your regular daily self: a fear that you won't be adequate enough to sustain a longer or deeper relationship, or even that you cannot *really* trust yourself with someone you're already involved with regularly, or trust him with your own most guarded secrets, sexual or otherwise.

Therefore the desire for novelty asserts itself in the compulsion toward constant sexual roaming and cruising. For some men, the search itself is satisfying; all agendas have been laid aside except for the sheer aggression of finding what you feel you want, or believe you deserve.

In the old days (pre-"Stonewall"), when any evidence of a queer relationship was an obvious revelation of who you were, compulsive gay cruising was "normal." It was too dangerous to do otherwise, and a constant stream of "tricks," or encounters, meant that your co-workers or relatives could not tie you to another man for very long. Today, we feel more judgmental toward sexual promiscuity, but we forget that the good thing about this kind of "shopping" is that it brings a great deal of exciting information to you. You see that there is a big world out there, filled with a number of guys having different viewpoints, interests, and feelings. This in itself can be amazingly fulfilling, and simply fun to explore.

11. The desire to take on another identity, way of being, or role. This seems to be a "classic" gay desire, in that so many of us have spent some time, admit it or not, either trying to be something we aren't—i.e., playing it "straight"—or hoping not to be seen for what we are. But we can also use this desire to empathize a lot. As we take on other identities, we can also see deeper into other people. Out of this desire can stem a whole personal history of protective coloration—some might call this simply lying, even if it was for your own survival—and various periods of "shape-shifting," that is, exploring other parts of yourself. One day you are a husband, and the next day you are not. One day you are a "normal" regular guy, and the next day you are living in a "movie," certainly a theatrical event (as romantic relationships usually are), one that you are producing and directing by yourself.

I could say that the phenomenon of transgenderism may come from this desire, but I'd get into a lot of hot water if I did. However, as I honestly believe there are some transgender elements within most of us, it plays into the desire I am describing here.

What I feel here, though, is that in our desire to take on another role, to easily become "spies" in other houses, we can also assume a personal need to acquire power through knowledge: we can see deeply into things, including the psyches of the men we are involved with.

In other words, our own Deeper Self is actually traveling through these psyches, physically and psychically, gathering an intimacy unknown to the regular "straight" world.

12. The desire to assert your own identity, after it has been repressed. This is the basic desire to tell the truth in a world that you may feel, by its very nature, is one of untruths, near truths, and plain lies. It is a large desire, and you may feel that in sexuality itself, a basic truth is being revealed: that your very real *physical* self, accompanied by your

Deeper Self, is leading you into more fundamental levels of truth you did not know.

13. The desire to lose control—safely. OK, here we are getting scarier, down to the deepest aspects of desire. Our own personal history, from our families to our religious backgrounds, has a role in this desire. What we want is to leave ourselves and let our own Deeper Self take over, as a participant and a witness. Extremely "good" sex usually involves this, but it can be scary too. Cults and cult-leaders use this, as do people within hierarchical religious settings. The Catholic oath of "poverty, chastity, and obedience" plays directly into it, but usually with the goal of good.

Sexual rituals that involve "mind games," such as erotic hypnotism and bondage, use this desire, with the main goal being to lose inhibitions. However, if you *are* aware of your own inhibitions, clearly in these situations you are not losing control at all, but are simply offering control to someone else. The real problem is negotiating that moment when you *have* lost control, and how to be safely led back to it.

In real life, these moments of losing control can be extremely erotic, too. They are often part of the scenario people pay for with prostitutes and hustlers, as New York's former governor Eliot Spitzer can attest. So, in these situations the challenges and dangers of the play between the erotic and the "real" can lead to an extreme turn on, risky as it is.

These risky excitements, in turn, become elements for huge amounts of our erotic imaginations. The risk brings with it a question of how to engage, release, subvert—enjoy!—and then restore your own autonomy and power.

14. The desire to control—safely. Here, as a religious metaphor, you are entering into the "God-structure" itself. By controlling sexual situations, you definitely enlarge yourself, and even "float" above them. You also find yourself responsible for these situations and it is a *big* responsibility. Our culture is extremely "starstruck." The person who is at the center of attention and excitement *is* the star. This is often expressed in the desire to be in control, but in taking on that role as the "top," to use that term again, you can, yourself, be repressing as much of your personality (especially a deeper need for the "innocence without roles" of love) as you are actually revealing.

Therefore it is important to allow yourself some time to reveal your own vulnerabilities, fears, and needs to be taken care of.

15. The desire to share control. To be in balance with the world, and the universe. To relinquish part of yourself, and bring in another self, a greater one due to this sharing. I will talk more about dealing with this important last desire in talking about desire and spirituality, and prayers of sex.

Some Fast Track Desires Not to Lose Track Of

Along with these basic desires though, we have other "fast-track" desires—and I don't want to dismiss them completely. They're important. You deal with them everyday; in fact, they color your life. Here they are, but possibly you can even come up with some of your own.

Basic horniness. OK, guy, here it is. Right in front of you! I can talk in abstractions until you slam this book closed, but you know as well as I do that sexual appetite is important. It can be frustrating—or lead to a lot of fun! And sex is, or should be, *fun*. It should be marvelous; it should be satisfying in ways that very few other things are, and one of the basic premises of this book is that sex + the deeper channels that sexuality works through, can be among the most satisfying, nourishing, and beautiful moments of your life.

Basic desire for security and status. We all like to know where we are going to sleep tonight, how we are going to eat, and how we stand in the eyes of our peers, friends, or families, either biological or "families of choice." The desire to fit in is very important, and often it gives way to the next desire.

Basic desire for recognition. Recognition inflates us. It also allows us to step outside ourselves and see ourselves nicely, from the standpoint of others. This unfortunately can become addictive and blinding, as anyone in a "celebrity" role can tell you. You can start to see yourself too much as a manufactured item, something that others have created and can just as easily destroy. This leads us to the next fast-track desire.

The desire to avoid shame. Recognition is the opposite of shame, but avoiding shame is extremely important for many people, especially if their childhood conditioning has been shaped by it. Shame makes you feel tiny, powerless, and worthless. Men ruled by shame never really grow up to become the person they could be: the person who gets to express himself in his larger desires—to assert his own identity, to tell the truth, and to assume the *real* power of his own Deeper Self.

Some Thinking for You

Have I left out a very personal desire that you feel you've been hiding? Is there some desire you'd like to acknowledge that you have not been acknowledging before? Externalizing these desires, bringing them to consciousness, is very important in the manly pursuit of desire and love. You don't have to share these with others, unless you really want to, but it's important to recognize them for yourself.

_____

_____

_____

_____

5 Finding The "Deeper Self"

In the past chapters, I spoke about the Deeper Self. It is impossible for me to talk about desire without bringing up this important concept, but I wanted to bring your attention to the Basic Desires before we talked at length about the Deeper Self. Why? Because desire, no matter how you explain it, is still pretty concrete. It's here and now, and most of you know that, especially if it's bothering you and you've been trying to control it. But the Deeper Self is a much more abstract, but important idea and it needs some time and space to deal with it fully.

First of all, what is the Deeper Self?

The Deeper Self is that part of you that remains with you your entire life. It contains your most secret feelings; we all have these feelings, even people ashamed to admit them. Desire, happiness, and most of your own *genuine* self-preservation are wrapped up in the Deeper Self, therefore it (sometimes I refer to *it* as "he") responds to the lies you have to tell about yourself, even the "necessary" lies. The Deeper Self is also the safe haven of your most imaginative being, the place where you are your most *you*. It is the guardian and companion of your greatest happiness, and certainly of those rare moments when you can be . . . well . . . *yourself.*

Your true, and real, self.

It is also that part of you that allows you to connect most *meaningfully* with others, and that keeps us centered. In other words, it is the inner gyroscope of our lives. It is therefore often strengthened by adversity and the knowledge that comes from adversity; not the cynicism that comes from it and the pain, but the genuine self-knowledge that lets us know that we have grown. The Deeper Self is illuminated, that is, brightened, by genuine support, not simply the standard mirrors of narcissism around us (which so much of our consumer society provides) but the support of loving friends and peers. I feel about the Deeper Self that it is an organic part of me that I cannot live without.

I have been blessed by its continuous presence in my life, and hope you will be too. But, like Peter Pan's shadow, it's easy to lose track of.

It's also hard to understand how such an innate *part* of you is still separate from you, until those moments when you unite with it. Most of what we call "religion" is a story of what we can see as humans being united with our Deeper Selves, then experiencing an intense change. Whether it is the story of Jacob wrestling with the angel who renames him Israel; Gautama finding Enlightenment as the Buddha; or the Hebrew Jesus of Nazareth becoming Christ, in each instance someone is being renamed (and identified) by being united with a Deeper Self. In each situation there is the Quest to find that thing that has been separated from us, and the moment that will change us.

(Note: the Deeper Self, then, can respond to a role, or a name change, but the Deeper Self is basically *you* beyond the roles and identities that we cling to, often, for security. The Deeper Self offers us a security beyond them.)

The Deeper Self as the "Lost" Soul

Is the Deeper Self then simply another term for the "soul"?

Yes, in that it is at the *core* of us. But *no*, in that so much of our concepts about the soul are dependent on you being on terms of "good behavior," and the bad consequences of deviating from "good behavior" which the Deeper Self can, in fact, work to protect you from. In other words, the Deeper Self allows you to stand up for yourself—for *you*—in a world that often rejects this. To the Deeper Self you are not simply loved for being the popular kid and "the best little boy in the world," but for being your real self, including some behaviors and attitudes others may not always approve of.

So, your Sunday school self is not what the Deeper Self is all about. But "he," or *it,* is about you being the best person *you* can be.

Most important, what I want you to know about the Deeper Self is that when you do see it as apart from the everyday working "guy" you became (the one who gets up in the morning and does things he might not want to do; for instance go to a job you don't like, or tell "social" lies, or pretend not to be interested in things you actually are interested in) . . . when you *are* able to connect with this Deeper Self on a *separate* but intimate level, then *he* (and definitely here I want to call him *he*) will definitely—

—*love* you.

I mean this. Yes, your Deeper Self, that center of your own feelings and longed-for innocence (and I'll talk a lot about that *innocence* in this book), as part of all of your most "spiritual" aspects, *will* love you.

But, the question I'm sure you're asking now is, "How do I connect with *him*, my Deeper Self, on a regular basis? How do I get to know this Deeper Self?"

There are many answers to that question, but one very approachable answer is: Through our *recognition* of the full range and depth of desire.

As for other ways? In the next chapter, I will talk about them, too.

CHAPTER 6

10 Distinct Ways to Connect with the Deeper Self

"All human wisdom is ourselves to know."

Baruch Spinoza

It is important to understand how to connect with your Deeper Self. Even living in the stressful city of New York I find moments to do it on a regular basis. And I look forward to times, places, and certainly people who allow me to do this.

1. Allow yourself moments to disengage, especially from pressures that are stressful, that keep you from feeling whole and undivided. Most of these pressures come from expectations you've built up either for yourself or others. I mean all sorts of expectations: social, professional, sexual, or even recreational. Disengagement means that you don't have to "get your money's worth" at all times. You don't have to optimize and maximize every moment of your life, but you do need to allow yourself time—even small amounts of it—to be disengaged from the pressures, problems, and obligations to be something other than yourself.

2. Become aware of your own "inner beauty," and allow this awareness to see the real beauty of others. This is difficult in our world where "image is everything," and control is paramount—in fact, can make the difference between you surviving or not. But it is important to see your individuality as opposed to the expectations of others. The Japanese have a word for the beauty of irregularity, the beauty of disfigurement and imperfection: *shibui*. In our marketing culture where so little of the inner you is allowed out, unless of course it is expedient, allowing yourself to see and revel in your own inner beauty and imperfections will bring you closer to the Deeper Self waiting for you.

I know that for many people even the concept of inner beauty is difficult to grasp. What is inner beauty? *It is the curiosity and desire for life that exceeds the difficulties and obstacles existence places in front of anyone.* It includes courage and real intelligence (that is, not simply the ability to play games), and a sense of radiating love, compassion,

19

and comfort. Realizing inner beauty also means, on an interpersonal basis, that you don't have to have obvious things "in common" with others to have satisfying relationships. There may be things not evident within the inner beauty of someone else. The thing "in common" is that you both want to know and share each other's value.

3. Have a moment of attachment to the natural world, the world of nature, as you disengage from electronics, video games, and the constant entertainments we use to keep us away from the Deeper Self. Also, realize that there is a nature that is a part of human nature—observe how people become human on a daily basis; this is part of the great drama of life. How people reveal small, but beautiful parts of themselves; try to become conscious and sensitive of this.

4. There are many ways of going inward to reach the Deeper Self. They include meditation, prayer, connecting through art or music, or writing (your own and others.) Pick a way that works for you, or use several.

5. Take up writing a journal. A journal is a book of your own feelings and observations. It differs from a diary in that you don't have to write in it every day, and you choose what you want to write. The important thing is that it allows you to see some of your thoughts and feelings externalized. It can include small drawings, clippings that interest you, and stuff that you feel are a part of your world. It can also become a "common book," that is a collection of quotes and thoughts from others that you find appealing and important to your own journey toward the Deeper Self. A journal can become extremely important. Everyone has moments of doubt and despair. At these times, a journal can save your life, when you see the progress you have made, where you've been, and what you are allowing yourself to see and know. So it's important not only to write in your journal, but also to read it from time to time. See what your thoughts have been, how they've changed and are growing.

6. Turn off the extraneous noise, the "tape" that goes on in your head repeating past problems, grudges, stresses, hurts, and insults. This is the baggage we all carry and that becomes part of our "story," a story that can take over and push out the beauty of connecting with the Deeper Self, which remains eternally fresh and renewing. I have a difficult time with this, and I know that many of us do as well. Meditation as a technique can help with this. Meditation does not simply focus the mind, but allows the mind to find places in the "tape" that are clear enough for the real you to come forward. And at this point, the "tape" stops.

7. Have a partner (or partners) in your Quest—you are both (or all) on the path to that "Sword in the Stone," to connecting with the Deeper Self. This partner will become an important intimacy in your life, and, I feel, a necessary one. It is very sad to me that so many outside, authentic intimacies are now impossible for most people. They may hope to find closeness with people they work with, then realize how limited this closeness is. Other avenues for intimacy are "12-Step" programs, but these, for the most part, do not recognize desires beyond the ones they are trying to control. There are also religious organizations, but they have their own, often tight boundaries and rules. So recognizing a partner (or partners) in the quest for the Deeper Self can become vital to you. The partner (or partners) may be sexual/romantic or not, but the depth of this relationship will be based on trust, and a willingness to be open about feelings you find difficult to share with many people. One of the interesting things about finding partners in your quest is that, like the "Sword in the Stone" story (which I will talk about later), once you find them, recognizing them can be amazingly easy: you will feel a naturalness, comfort, and calm with them. And also the excitement of recognition, of being truly revitalized.

8. Experience an emotional, spiritual, and even physical "cleanse and refresh" period often. Even everyday, if you can. This means not only *disengagement*, but introducing something that makes you feel more open and happier than before. It can be ten minutes of reading something that has a profound value to you, of physical exercise even if only a walk, as well as practicing simple mindfulness. What is mindfulness? It is awareness without judgment. You are looking at things without describing them as "good," "bad," "beautiful" or "ugly." You are simply allowing yourself to see them as whole experiences.

9. *Sexual meditation*. People often feel that sex is as far from meditation as they can get, but this is not true. You can be mindful during sex: of your partner's physical body and what is behind it, of the great vista you are sharing with one another, and of the personal history and stories you are both sharing even without speaking. Later you will find a chapter on "Sex as Story, Narrative, Ritual, and Promise." It will go more into sex as meditation and where it can take you.

10. Birth and death. We are being reborn and dying constantly, just as the earth itself goes through its seasonal cycles. Realize the depth of feeling behind these natural occurrences, that every change we go through has a seasonal reaction. With every new step forward, every birth, comes the shedding of some kind of "womb," and the protections that have hindered us from taking the step; with every growth comes a change that will end in a "death" of its own; and with every end, there is a glimpse of a beginning.

Some Important Notes About the Deeper Self

On disengagement: Stresses and pressures can include friendships that have obvious "strings attached," and you are probably aware of them. When your friends make it plain that you are there to augment their sense of importance, that there are all sorts of status games going on, that you are only there for "good behavior," and they can drop you at any moment, and make that plain too—these kind of people separate you from your Deeper Self.

This does not mean that you have to choose people who are "flakes" as friends, but when you feel other people are robbing you of something that is important—the very oxygen you need to breathe and feel good— then disengage from them.

What is it that you want to offer others, and your Deeper Self? Your creativity, your goodness, the essence of you that you have been hiding for so long. Understand that all of art—and most human activity—has been done basically as an offering to a higher energy and Consciousness that performs through the Universe. Once you understand this, you can connect with this energy and Consciousness (of which you are definitely a part), and in it find your Deeper Self.

One thing is certain: this energy and consciousness—and they are very much bound together in one package—has evolved and can be seen in our deepest ideas, feelings, and teachings. All of our religious feelings come out of it, but often they are at war with basic human aggression and needs for defenses. But the primary religious feeling is a return to the Deeper Self, and the even Greater Self, the one Consciousness that unites us all.

This Deeper Self allows you to become centered and in balance.

I have described it as the "gyroscope" of our being: it allows us to right ourselves after failures, falling, and disasters. It allows us to withstand rejection, and pain. We may put a face on it as that of Jesus or any other religious figure, or *not* put a face on it while still connecting with it. But I feel that it is every human's birthright, and, very important, it includes that most luminous blessing: the knowledge of who we really are.

Drugs and Rituals

Some people have used drugs like peyote, marijuana, or L.S.D. to connect with the Deeper Self. Personally, I feel that this only connects us with the outer shell of it, or a cosmetic face of it. It is "groovy," and "cosmic," and sometimes fun to do, and at other times disastrous (as in those "bad trips"). But the greatest "trip" comes from practices that bring you on one hand closer to your Deeper Self, and on the other hand unites you with others who are seeking evidence of that Self and finding it, too.

Sometimes these others may not even be alive, but we are also contacting with their spirits. They can be dead friends or relatives from the past, whose presence now suddenly become evident to us. In my book *How to Survive Your Own Gay Life*, I talk about having sexual connections with dead friends who have died of AIDS. That is, a connection that is so deep that it veers onto the *realities* of sex, and sex is very real. What I am saying here is that there is a connection with the spirit that lives on, which is engaging with our Deeper Self, and also lives within it.

The Deeper Self does not die, and yet I cannot speak of it in the usual terms of ghosts or "souls" who live on. But, just as batteries contain a stored energy that can be recharged from a larger source of energy, so does this Self; it can connect with that larger energy of the Universe. Part of that connection is through understanding without defenses, perceiving a basic sense and beauty that is being offered to us. One way of partaking of these offerings is through art and literature (and I am a great fan of both).

Another way is through nature, and also, very much, through that important recognition of the basic *humanity* inside people.

I live in New York and I am aware of this all the time: the great drama inside this amazing city; the courage needed to deal with its stresses, the gifts strangers give me all the time with their tiny moments of kindness that I invite, and the small parts of themselves they reveal even within a congested urban bustle. Walt Whitman understood this over a hundred and fifty years ago, and it is still possible to share it. But you can share it in other places, in small towns as well as larger ones, any place where you emerge from your own fears enough to see it.

I have called these the "Buddha moments," when someone has come out of him or herself to offer me some small courtesy, stepping aside so I can pass on a crowded subway platform, opening the door for me, reminding me that I forgot a glove. These moments include what I call the "unbidden gifts," ones that are simply offered to you. It is important to see them and never undervalue them.

It is also important to see your own desires within them, as a part of the Deeper Self. When kindness is offered to you without asking, they are sharing their own Self with you and opening up a space for the greatness of desire, even if the space is not sexual but is working on a more subtle, and perhaps more nourishing level.

Thoughts for You

Have you had a moment of real contact or connection with your Deeper Self? Can you talk about it in words? Please express your thoughts here.

_____

_____

_____

7   The Search for Authenticity

One of the great quests of adulthood is the search for authenticity; that is, the desire to attain what (and who) we really are. This desire runs on a parallel track with the quest for finding a place in a community, that is, your "role" in life. This search for authenticity is behind the unsettling power—the sheer "awesomeness"—of what we call spiritual feelings, because these feelings contain, in their energy and grip on us, the core of this search. I will speak about spiritual feelings, desire, and attaining authenticity a lot in this book.

Each generation as it identifies itself redefines this search for authenticity, often within either the stated (or public) goals of the generation, or as an unstated but tacitly acknowledged agenda or plan. The World War II generation found its identity in the idea of "national character," whether you were an American, British, French, German, or Italian. Members of minority groups (like blacks or Native Americans in the U.S.) were basically treated as invisible, or (like Jews, Jehovah's Witnesses, gypsies, or homosexuals in Europe) detestable and marked for destruction because they did not fit into the "national character."

My own generation, the post-war baby boomers, born after the atomic bomb ended World War II with a huge destructive flash, believed very much in its own "authenticity." We wanted a return to an idealized innocence that the bomb and the universal threat of mass destruction had destroyed. The next group of younger people known as "Generation X" has searched for security in an increasingly insecure world, where parents no longer stay together, there is no lifetime job security, and the idea of "home" and "home town" exist only as nostalgia.

Back to my generation of the baby boomers, we wanted this innocence to be affirmed and strengthened through generosity toward others (civil rights, the anti-war movement and feminist movements, the emergence of gay liberation) as well as intelligence. Many of us had gone to college, read the classic books, and wanted to join our intellects to our sensual selves.

What we missed, I feel, was the discipline the earlier generation had, which had fought in World War II and had lived through the Great Depression.

The "post-boomers" are seeking their own authenticity in a world made painfully self-conscious by media saturation, and flattened by consumerism. Today, you are what you buy and consume, but is that what you *really* are?

Younger people are looking desperately for something to believe in beside themselves, even though consumerism has told them that they, as "valued" customers, are at the center of everything.

I know you don't believe that, because you are reading this book. You want to connect with your own authenticity, that we can locate within the Deeper Self, that is the authentic aspect of you that makes you feel alive, spontaneous, and happy—and also secure in your own self-knowledge. No matter what generation you come from, this search for authenticity is still the most important search in adult life. It answers the questions of who you are, what you are here for, what do you want, and how you will achieve it?

Be certain of one thing: Our desires stand behind all of these questions, as they contain the most powerful keys to our own Deeper Self.

8 The Search for Authenticity as "the Sword in the Stone"

> "And therein stuck a fair sword naked by the point, and letters were written in gold about the sword that said thus: 'WHOSO PULLETH OUT THIS SWORD OF THIS STONE IS RIGHTWISE KING BORN OF ALL ENGLAND' . . . . So when all the masses were done all the lords went to behold the stone and the sword . . . but none might stir the sword nor move it."
>
> Sir Thomas Mallory, *King Arthur and His Knights*

A perfect mythological metaphor for the search for authenticity is "the Sword in the Stone" story which lies at the heart of the Arthurian legends, those powerful, ancient stories about King Arthur and the Knights of the Round Table that have captivated people for centuries. "The Sword in the Stone" represents the simple but great Quest (and challenge) of any human lifetime, the one which reveals the identity of a special person.

You.

Remember, in this search your "real" identity has been kept a secret, but it will be revealed once this Quest has been fulfilled. To fulfill the Quest, you must negotiate a path that sometimes feels strange, futile, hopelessly testing, and frustrating. Yet, oddly enough, once the Quest itself has been fulfilled, the longed-for goal at its end—the realization of your own identity—will seem . . . well . . . *natural.* Even *easy,* that's the only word for it, after so much effort.

And, at that point, the ultimate reality of who you are cannot be denied.

In the Arthurian legend, a beautiful sword imbedded in a large stone appeared suddenly in the churchyard of the greatest cathedral in the town. All of the most powerful knights tried to extract the sword from the stone, but none could. One day young Arthur, still in his teens, was sent alone to retrieve the sword of Sir Kay, the younger son of Sir Ector, the knight who had raised young Arthur since the boy's own father, the powerful King Uther Pendragon, could not claim him due to the questionable circumstances of Arthur's birth. Arthur had never been told who his real father was. He had been brought up without privilege of any sort, in the guise of a stable boy.

Spotting the Sword in the Stone in the deserted courtyard, Arthur approached it and then without thinking, casually drew it out.

When he brought it to Sir Kay and Sir Ector, they knew immediately what the sword was, and that they could no longer hide Arthur's real identity from him: He was the son of a powerful king. And although Arthur's path toward the Sword had been difficult and certainly "irregular," having been raised to be a menial, without any kind of pomp, privilege, or recognition of his lineage, pulling the Sword from the Stone had been only too easy.

I feel that we are all meant to pull our own "Sword out of the Stone."

This is our meaning and destiny in life, to accomplish the work and goals that will give us an identity. But so many things stand in the way of this: Our defensive egoism, our ingrained feelings of shame; and our feelings, deep inside, of doubt and unworthiness often masked by cynicism and emotional coldness. Still the Stone, in the role of a challenge that will reveal itself to us, is present. And the Sword, both the reward and the key to our actual identity, is present as well. Therefore, when we become our *real* selves, united with our Deeper Selves, you find that the Sword slides easily from the Stone.

Having a "pursuit" helps. By a pursuit, I mean to become the thing that you want to be, whether it is an artist, a writer, a doctor, a scientist, a business or tech person—or a pioneer, explorer, activist, lover, or husband. This "pursuit" definitely becomes part of your Quest, so that at a certain point you'll find that you *have* become what you really wanted to be. The pursuit and the Quest are both parts of fulfilling that idea we call "identity" which answers the question of who you are.

But please be aware of this: fulfilling that Quest—pulling your own particular sword out of the Stone—is very significant, but only *one* step toward uniting you with that longed for entity of your own Deeper Self.

Work for You to Think About

Can you name what was your own Quest? What test brought you to realize exactly who you were? Was it leaving home? Your first job? Your first romantic interest? Or was it another important challenge that you met, but stepping up to it was in no way easy?

_____

_____

_____

What pursuits did you have that brought you to this present knowledge?

_____

_____

_____

CHAPTER 9

After "the Sword in the Stone": Desire as Life Saving

Even after you have pulled your sword from the stone, and have fulfilled the Quest of your own identity, you may still find times when it's difficult not to give in to despair. Many of us know this. Maybe it's simply a part of modern human life, one of the shadows cast by the burdens of consciousness itself, a shadow that people who deal with depression on a regular basis understand. But how do you keep from giving in to despair? Or, to really bring the question to its ultimate conclusion: How do you keep from killing yourself when you feel that your time has run out, and your own problems and the depression under them are finally pulling you down?

Americans are now killing themselves in far greater numbers than committing homicides. Not than I'm ever in favor of people killing others, but suicide has become a greater danger to many sectors of our society than homicide. This is especially true among people above the age of 25. For people below 25, suicide has become the third largest cause of death after automobile injuries and homicides. However, as you climb up in age, auto injuries become less common, as do homicides, and suicide numbers leap off the page. In the year 2010, a staggering 39,518 people killed themselves in the U.S, as opposed to 14,748 homicides.

So what I want to talk about in this chapter is very simple:

Can desire, within its healthiest components, keep you alive?

Sigmund Freud wrote about the *Thanatos* or Death Drive versus the *Eros*, or Life Drive. We see this hand-to-hand, and often hand-to-throat conflict between the two drives all the time. History is written in terms of it. Repressing the Life Drive, squeezing it to fit into rigid religious, social, political, career, and military agendas results in the "thought fascism" you see in many cultures and countries where normal human warmth and eroticism are violently rejected and a very real, often lethal agenda of cruelty is encouraged as "normal."

One result of this is a population alienated from itself. People stop talking openly to each other, and stop feeling sympathetic and empathetic toward one another as well. Since sympathy and empathy are very normal aspects of human interaction—going back to our needs for warmth and contact—another kind of relationship is substituted, that of the repressive agenda itself. A beautiful example are kids who will do anything to become "popular," acceptable, or accepted. During the Nazi period in Germany, these kids would turn their parents in if they felt that by doing this they would gain acceptance from the Nazi regime. They would prove to be "normal" Aryans. Most bullying comes from the same source: the desire to be seen as "acceptable," "regular," or "normal," when often bullies don't feel at all that way inside.

We find this in the queer world too, where gay men feel that in order to be "acceptable" to their friends (or to mainstream society), they also have to closely fit a mold that is not what they really are. To do otherwise is extremely threatening to them. Much of this comes from the homophobic poisoning that I will speak about soon, but basically it means cutting off a great part of themselves and denying their own histories. They are terrified of growing up and growing old. They accept the shallow commercialism of so much of what is now called the "gay world" as the total boundaries of their own.

Being able to see deeper and ask questions is not "cool."

Also not cool: having genuine contact with that part of you that loves you not *un*conditionally (this means you do have a *conscience*), but with a wisdom that you need to stay alive: I'm talking here about your Deeper Self again. The Deeper Self, like the angel who wrestled with Jacob and then re-named him Israel, loves you. He (or "It" because "it" does not really have a gender) does not want you to go down for the count. This means that no matter how many times you think or feel that you've failed, your own survival is absolutely important. But in order to survive, you have to allow yourself time to recharge, to recoup your own value in situations that often rob you of it.

This book is about desire in its various beautiful forms, but the most important form desire can take is *life saving*. It is, simply stated, the most approachable part of the Eros drive. And this in itself is important to understand, no matter how people in their constant need for self-righteousness try to denigrate it. A very important part of desire and sexuality itself is their ability to take you out of the closed situation of your own life, and bring you to a larger "vista," a beautiful place where your own deeper narratives and feelings can be expressed in a way that is organic to you.

It is extremely important to understand this: that these feeling are organic, that you can redirect them into healthier scenarios if that is either necessary or appropriate for you (and I will talk about that later, also) but denying them completely is not only unhealthy but can even be lethal.

10 Defanging Desire, Or, At Least Sucking the Poison Out

This is an important concept:

As many of you have already found out, desire is a *poisonous* word in our culture.

Sex is used constantly, blatantly, to sell everything, but desire itself is thrown down the church stairs, reminding me of that wonderful scene at the end of *The Graduate* when young Benjamin Braddock (played by Dustin Hoffman) uses a cross ripped from the wall to jam the door of the church, locking his enemies within. Now Benjamin and Elaine Robinson (Katherine Ross), the girl he desires so much and who represents everything that he yearns for—normalcy, innocence, and authenticity—can escape her parent-imposed, wedding-cake-perfect wedding.

Desire is thrown down the church stairs, locked away in prisons, becomes the stuff of investigations into pornography, blasphemy, obscenity, subversion, *per*version, and the gratifying, self-righteous crusades behind many of the most horrifying elements of violence and war. Why is that?

Because desire returns us to views of forbidden territory: things which should be kept secret at the very least, even in our "post privacy" period in which there are no more secrets. Everyday we hear about ordinary men and women who've been unmasked publicly as "predators," "perverts," or "weirdos," usually for having some forbidden inclination exposed against their will.

Therefore, desire is also seen as the basis of uncontrollable impulses, at a time in which control is more and more necessary for "Security" reasons. To keep the world secure, and in control, is a huge industry, and it is terrifying how easy it is to become caught up in it. Anything that puts you out of control, including asking the wrong person out for a date, can have definite punitive consequences. We are now on witch-hunts, looking for deviants in every computer hard drive. It is a reminder that back in 1950s America, during the Cold War, sexual deviance of any sort (meaning you were somehow different from TV's

"Ozzie and Harriet" or "Leave It to Beaver" model) was often associated with political subversion.

You were a "queer" and also a "Red." Strangely enough, the times when the two did coincide were vastly outnumbered by when they didn't. Conservative preachers, Bible-thumpers, and Marine Corp drill sergeants could be "queer as 3-dollar bills" and often, happily, found themselves in remarkably comfortable positions to hide it. This led to a "culture of the closet" whose primary purpose was never to let out your own real "identity," that is, some of the most fundamental parts of you.

But, equally strangely enough, even in cases of Bible-thumpers and Marine Corp drill sergeants, desire no matter how hidden often revealed certain aspects of themselves. For instance, you kept an immaculate house filled with antiques. You allowed yourself to like ballet, or opera, or military history, or Friday night wrestling on TV—but you were always scared. So much so that your own *real* feelings—the ones sheltered inside your Deeper Self—were being smothered on a daily basis.

Although desire is somewhat coming out of the closet, with suburban heterosexual housewives admitting that "a little bondage" might turn them on, the more private and forbidden aspects of it are still shameful to a lot of people. Here I want, though, to bring up a big distinction:

The difference between desire and plain *horniness*:

Horniness is physical. It's hormonal. Kids exhibit it almost 24/7 from the age of, say, 14 to about . . . well, that depends on the kid. Some men never really outgrow it, and that libidinal energy drives them much of their lives.

Desire though is infinitely deeper. It is part of the engine that may run horniness, but it can also be extremely perverted by it. I am talking here in the case of rape, exploitative sex, and *feelingless* sex.

(Please note: I want to make a distinction between feelingless sex and what I call "historyless" sex—that is, sex with strangers—or *anonymous* sex. Neither of these later two sexual encounters has to be feelingless. Feelingless sex does not take into account the feelings, well-being, and implications of a sexual act on the object of arousal. Rape is definitely feelingless sex, engined by aggression and extreme, pent-up anger. It does not take into account the feelings of the victim. This is also true of exploitative sex with minors; I will talk about that at a later place in this book.)

34

CHAPTER 11

Surviving Homophobic Poisoning

I think it's important here to bring up the long-term effects of homophobia on not only your life but the lives of the people around you, whether they identify as sexually straight or not. We live in a culture, atmosphere, and world emotionally and psychologically poisoned by homophobia—that is a deeply ingrained fear of what is culturally unacceptable, put into conveniently sexual or gender-defined terms. In other words, what in other eras was considered blasphemous, sinful, unnatural, abnormal, subversive, unpatriotic—I could go on with lots of other pejoratives—is now grouped under the rubric of "queer." And in many ways this is more terrifying because it hits at the very foundation of everyone's deepest "secret room."

Unlike racial or ethnic differences, *queerness* is so shot through the deeper organs and muscles of human experience, is such a part of our own universal histories, that just exposing these secrets in any way and in any place, be it a fundamentalist church in America or Uganda, a mosque in Afghanistan, or a Marine Corp unit on patrol in Iraq, and people still freeze dead, even in this age of gay marriage, the end of Don't Ask Don't Tell, and the more recent appearance of gay sports stars and celebrities.

So how do you deal with this in your own life—and how do you recognize it in the lives of your friends, gay and straight? The first thing to understand is how deeply homophobic poisoning has affected queer men especially. So many of the characteristics we too often see in them have roots in homophobic poisoning: Self-rejection and the real rejection of other gay men. Bitchiness, snobbery, racism, or class-pretensions as a defense. Endless competitiveness with other queer men, coupled with a painfully wearing self-consciousness. Smug self-abnegation (what I call the "Best Little Boy in the World" syndrome), coupled with fears of placing themselves in any kind of genuine risk. Also, quick-trigger anger and explosiveness, found too often in tandem with emotional coldness and a constant disengagement of deeper feelings.

In straight-identified men, we see homophobic poisoning in the fear of closeness with other men, and their intense emotional clinging to women as the only source of a "soul warmth" in their lives—except for the more acceptable one of organized religion (God, Jesus, etc.). We also see it in an intimacy with daughters but not with sons, except when fathers and sons can bond over sports, hunting, or other "manly" competitive pursuits. In this way, homophobic poison is passed from one dysfunctional generation to the next. This leads to the primary bonding between fathers and sons found in sports mania—both Junior and Dad wearing the same Yankees pinstripes or Cubs colors—or by completing joint projects and tasks, such as learning to use a tire jack or a hammer. In many families, Dad is so disengaged that the only role he has left is that of the "provider," or in modern terms, the one who "takes care" of the kids' Visa bills at the end of the month.

It is no secret that now that sex has come almost completely out of the closet, homophobia has been released as well. The pervading influence of homophobic poisoning is hard to gage, although the results of it are not, whether we are talking about the huge number of gay or "questioning" teens who either attempt suicide every year or succeed at it, or the number of marriages (gay or straight) that fail because one or both of the partners have become completely dysfunctional because of it. The roots of homophobia are still being debated. Is it a primal fear of castration (seeing the "passive" male in anal sex as being a "eunuch" or castrated); fear or hatred of women and their "submissive" role; fear of weakness or powerlessness; or simply just a need to label outsiders as "queer"?

But the poison leaches into our speech and thoughts: Something you hate "sucks," or is "sucky"—a reference to fellatio. When you are in an inferior position you say, "I'm fucked," or "I just got fucked." Kids say, "That's so *gay*!" to mean that they hate anything that exposes them to ridicule. Queers are now the bogymen, jokers, devils, subversives, villains (in countless animated movies aimed at kids), and/or the stooges of the world.

A more insidious effect of homophobic poisoning though has resulted in the deep "anti-maleism" found in our culture. Maleism (and its opposite anti-maleism) is not the same thing as male chauvinism, the belief that men and their attitudes are definitely superior to women or gays. Maleism is simply upholding the images and exposing the deeper natural feelings of males.

We find anti-maleism in the attitude that any kind of support for men and their feelings is essentially "queer." And that the male body, especially the male *nude* body, is something to be shunned, especially by other men. There is now a huge amount of male body shame and prudery in American culture, despite the fact that homoeroticism, (geared always ostensibly to female consumers), is rampantly evident in advertising and the media. You especially see this on beaches where women and girls wear as little as they can get away with, and men and boys are wearing bathing suits that would be considered prim even back in Victorian times.

For men to show their bodies on the beach, or even during sports, is too "queer," too "gay." Basketball players now wear shorts that extend below their knees; forty years ago, basketball shorts *were* short: *really* short. Some of this has come from ghetto attitudes: in the black underclass, to expose your body meant that you were now "stuff," that is, as a man, you were fuckable. This was especially seen in prisons where black inmates feared getting a "rep" for being physically vulnerable. The flip side of this were men who intentionally wore their pants as far down as possible, exposing their butts. The subsequent message was: "I'm showing this to the other guys, and God help them if they look at it." So "booty"-showing clothes were an invitation to a confrontation; they showed exactly where the boundaries were, and what would happen if you crossed them.

"Junk" Fears

Anti-maleism has resulted in the currently fashionable term for male genitalia: a guy's "junk." The penis and testicles are revolting; they are things to be scorned, by regular guys and normal men. Men of course were always interested in each other's dicks as they sized each other up in locker rooms: it was a part of human curiosity. But any kind of interest in junk shows you are queer, you play on the losing team, and there is no other way to put it. Part of the denigration of the genitals as "junk" is that they can also get a guy into trouble: the dick (and desire itself) needs to be controlled at all times; there is no place for these feelings in the corporate or business world; in a bland social world that essentially castrates men for the sake of "adulthood." Here the penis *is* junk; it is part of the "boy world," that aspect of maleness that men always carry with them. And it is about as welcome as a smoker at a health food convention.

As you can see, even in the time of the popularity of "Ellen" and the two guys on "Modern Family," for queer men to announce our presence in the world in many areas—whether in the U.S. or out of it—is still risky, as homophobic poison relentlessly leaches in. As playwright and AIDS activist Larry Kramer has put it: "We're still a population of people tragically unrepresented by power." Chronic homophobic poisoning is part of this hiding, part of this fear of power.

Fighting Homophobic Poisoning

How can you deal with homophobic poisoning?

First by admitting it exists, and that it effects all men, queer or not, whether they want to admit it or not. One of the sad aspects of homophobic poisoning is the denial surrounding it—even admitting that it exists and effects you, means that you have now "gone over to the other side." You are definitely on shaky ground—no longer on "regular guy" territory. You are admitting there's a problem and for many men trying to blend into an acceptable, working environment, this is terrifying. They are admitting they are a "part of the problem" by simply recognizing it. They are saying that no matter where they stand sexually, they are "queer" enough to be counted as victims. Anyone who lived through the AIDS crisis realized that AIDS—the disease most American lawmakers and policy makers could not even mention for the first decade of this horror—and "queer" became synonymous. So you had to jump as far away from both as possible, unless you were willing to live with the consequences.

Luckily, a huge number of people decided that they had no choice: *Silence* did *equal Death*. On one hand AIDS did push a lot of men even deeper into the closet, but on the other it brought another group of them completely *out*. But this did not mean that they were free of homophobic poisoning. What they started to understand is that, like racism itself and sexism against women, it is much deeper than we think.

So the first thing is to admit that homophobic poisoning is still constantly around us, and it affects our total lives, emotionally and psychologically, as well as sexually and physically. Despite the media's hard-sell use of sex, we live in very sexually-negative times. Even horny teens now equate sex with abuse, disease, destruction, violence, lies, and punishable sinfulness. The ideas that sex is natural, has a heart-felt dimension, and is a bonding element between people, have been lost in the hard-sell shuffle.

So the first thing is to admit that the poison is there.

And then to try to identify its results; to see them clearly.

You may be able to see it in the relationships you had with your family, when a favorite aunt, uncle, or cousin told you that you and your male partner or husband were welcome "just not around our kids."

Or a boss told you to "keep your personal stuff out of your work."

Or you realized that it was impossible for you to have the deeper relationship you wanted with another man, because to do so would be too "public." Perhaps you realized this when you and another man walked into a suburban shopping mall, and you felt tenser. You were not sure of what moves to make together. You became self-conscious about any kind of touching, or even looking at one another.

Even after the advent of gay marriage, many married gay men still find places where they fear announcing that their partner is another male—in other words, they, as a man, have a "husband." There are still places where this announcement can be embarrassing, humiliating, or possibly even explosive, and they are too afraid of the results.

After admitting that the poison is there, get involved. Join a group or organization that is fighting for lgbt rights, or a church that is gay-inviting; or consciously seek out people who understand your place in the world. Understand that fighting homophobic poisoning is worth the effort. A lot of men were made so toxic by it, for so long, that even fighting it never occurred to them. They felt that this fight was somebody else's. They could imagine fighting for the environment or abused pets, but not for themselves. This has really damaged their relationships with other people, especially the intimate partners in their lives. There are still tens of millions of men and women in America and the rest of the world who are still very much in the closet. This is hard for many younger people today even to understand, but it's true.

One reason why they stay in the closet is that they have convinced themselves that the image others have of them will be irreparably damaged by exposing themselves as gay or bisexual. Their neighbors or families will never see them in the same light once they make the decision to come out.

The unfortunate side of this is that too often the decision will be made for them; they will be caught in some "compromising" situation and others will learn about them in a negative way. This has happened to ministers and politicians caught in police stings, blackmail schemes, or on the basically privacy-less Internet. Suddenly their families, wives, co-workers and friends do find out, in what is often seen as a complete breach of trust and faith. Their "significant others," as well as the less significant ones, feel utterly betrayed, with no understanding that homophobic poisoning permeates society so deeply that many people are still too paralyzed by it to "come out."

Men especially in these situations need a community behind them, and sometimes do find themselves joining the gay or lgbt community itself. But even in their eventual coming out, they are a long way from understanding the depth and effects of homophobic poisoning, how it has affected and shrunk their lives, how it has distorted the feelings they have about themselves, and also the people they love.

Thoughts for You

What are your feelings about homophobic poisoning? Have you experienced it first hand, or is this a new concept for you?

_____

_____

_____

_____

_____

12 What's Inside You?: Sex as Story, Narrative, Ritual, and Promise

C H A P T E R

Old question, but let's ask it once again.

What's the sexiest part of your body?

OK, it's a hard one. Some men are even convinced that they don't have a "sexiest" part, but probably down the line you've heard somebody say that you do. In that case, maybe you're convinced it's your dick, chest, butt, shoulders, stomach or maybe even your face. I'm not going to argue with you here, if this is what you know.

But suppose you don't know it?

Suppose you had to learn it afresh, like you decided you needed to unlearn all the things that are holding you back sexually, emotionally, psychologically, and also simply as a feeling person.

So let's get to the real answer.

Your imagination. The imagination is where sexual fulfillment begins, and it's what we try the hardest to repress.

Why is that? Because it is, literally, bigger than you are. It is that place where all of the various hidden "yous" are stored, waiting to come out. You as an infant, as a child, as an adolescent, as a questioning young adult, and as a man dealing with both your own maturing process and the doubts and fears that go with it. The imagination is this living file we keep within us, filled with our stories, histories, tales, myths, and the rituals and promises that we want to see made, enacted, and kept.

It is, in short, the richest, most delicious, and voluptuous part of ourselves.

And most people are scared to death of it.

That is why we keep coming up with paltry excuses and substitutes for it, like third-rate Hollywood "sagas" of teenage vampires, "action heroes," and, strangely, in the twenty-first century, the spreading, dangerous, often highly commercialized "faiths" of religious literalism, like Christian, Moslem, and Jewish fundamentalism. But I'm not going to dwell on that. Let's get right to the point:

Spirituality—one of the great hot topics of the moments, something everyone from whistle-clean politicians to NFL stars with their mega-salaries attest to—what is it, how do we get to it, and how are we united with it?

Spirituality is that psychic space where the human imagination works on its deepest, most questing, and (for many) most satisfying level. It is that place where we see ourselves larger than our actual daily selves and go to connect with our own "personal narratives" (I will speak more about this later). It is also so connected *sexually* to us that separating one (sex) from the other (the Spirit) is both extremely potent, and, for many people, extremely dangerous.

This is the reason why orthodox (or fundamentalist) religion desperately needs to control sexuality, because sexuality and spirituality flow into one another like tributaries of the same river of human consciousness, about which I have spoken earlier. Somewhere in human prehistory, as consciousness emerged from the developing human brain, with it came a recognition of the figures we now call "God," or Spirit, as well as sexuality. The first art objects made by humans were fertility figures celebrating sexuality (female figures) and hunting (often animal or fierce male) figures celebrating the male need for expressing aggression, control, and power. At a later point, as consciousness became more refined, both figures became combined in a male-and-female god figure celebrating power and its own deeper sacred source, sexuality.

As humans started to live in the first cities in the Fertile Crescent, Mesopotamia (now Iraq), consciousness started to see interesting relationships between various figures of power: Ishtar (or Astarte) the Mesopotamian goddess (many of whose priests were male prostitutes) was the goddess of sex *and* war. Enki was the god of winds, storms, and of both life-giving rain and potent male sperm. In the midst of this environment of sexuality and spirituality, Abraham, who lived in Mesopotamia among the Chaldeans, called forth as his own "father-God" a force he connected with inside himself, unapproachable to all except his own offspring, "the children of Abraham." Abraham's god was ostensibly monotheistic (the early Hebrews actually did worship many of the ancient Mesopotamian gods as well as Jehovah), and who imposed upon his followers a series of rules that also included boundaries on behavior and sexuality.

(As a historical aside, the Mesopotamians themselves were known to be avidly homophobic, to differentiate themselves from some of their tribal neighbors who used homosexual relations as a means of controlling population. With limited fertile land even in the Fertile Crescent and endless fighting over it, controlling population, even back then, was important.)

These boundaries on behavior and sexuality were later codified, set down, and ended up as the famous Levitican laws, most notorious of which was the one condemning to death homosexual activities among men. Of course the question is still: What is a man "who lies with a man as with woman" actually doing? Is he engaged in temple prostitution, as many men who worked for Ishtar did? Is he actively in love with another man (or men), or simply using another man "as a woman," as many men in coercive prison situations do?

In other words, is one man brutalizing another—and the Old Testament is rife with rape and brutality—taking him against his will, raping him, as men were known to do with women?

Or, is one man actually expressing tenderness and the full power of his erotic imagination to another?

Whatever was going on in ancient biblical times, the Levitican laws will be used by politicians and religious leaders as long as an easily gullible public is willing to be influenced by them. I hope the readers of this book are not among that public. In other words, you are thinking for yourself, but if you are still bugged by Levitican problems—or were—I hope you'll continue reading anyway.

Intimates of the Sacred

For thousands of year, before the early Christian church condemned them, certain men and women followed a path known as becoming "sacred intimates." These were people who engaged with others sexually, and who were paid for sex. This payment was seen as a form of a temple offering, like tithing; it was also considered a "tax" given directly to the gods. To our eyes these temple "intimates" were "sex workers," or prostitutes, but they also had a holy mission.

These men and women (the "sacred intimates," or Intimates of the Sacred) quickly understood the power of either repressing or directing the naked energy of sacred spirituality/sexuality—going to extremely powerful places either through sexual intimacy, or by stopping it. They learned that they could consciously direct both of these energy sources, the secret, frighteningly hidden sacred and the sexual, so that they could be "switched" from one to the other, or powerfully combined. The most obvious example of repressing one's sexual nature would be a lifetime of strict celibacy, a course rare in ancient times but which later became institutionalized by the Catholic Church, in a stroke of "genius" by which the church could completely protect itself from outside influences: its primates, teachers, and workers were now either married to God Himself, or the Church herself, and, as in every marriage, outsiders would be barred while very powerful secrets were kept within.

Earlier the ancient Hebrews in Roman-occupied Palestine developed a faction of believers known as Essenes, whose young men often roamed into the wilderness to practice celibacy and prolonged fasting. In this wild environment, the two practices of withholding sex and food easily produced an effect of intense emotional "nakedness"—*ecstasy*. Hallucinations accompanied moments of spiritual awakening, and a bonding among them of life-and-death strength. They also practiced daily water immersions, not easy in a desert country, as a way of producing ritual cleanliness. By repressing sexuality and inviting light-headedness from hunger, by practicing a desire for physical cleanliness (remember "the desire to recover or assume [re-gather] innocence": first of the basic desires) this bonding of a group imagination was lifted up to the heavens where it was strengthened through a sharing of an intensely personal and powerful *narrative*: the Sacred one, the Father and his Son, abandoned, who had to claim his own name and relationship to God, amidst the revelation of Evil as temptation and betrayal: political, personal, and sexual.

(For more information about the power of these desert revelations, due to fasting and celibacy, please see Elaine Pagels's *Beyond Belief, The Secret Gospel of Thomas*, Vintage Books, 2004, page 100.)

All of this appeared in the wilderness, among these young Essenes who would return to the villages and cities of Palestine and preach what they had seen and felt out alone with each other. The Essenes produced charismatic figures, most probably among them John the Baptist, as well as Jesus and his followers. (That Jesus was an Essene has long been argued, but not proven.) They were able to work under the political extremes of secrecy and Roman and Hebrew repression, as well as use one of the most potent weapons in the human emotional arsenal: the need for unconditional love and the desire to maintain "virtuousness": that is, of being "politically" correct, on the side of righteousness, and "in the know," as far as which rules *authentically* apply and which do not.

Our Need for the "Personal Narrative" and Its Place in Love

Humans have a built-in need to establish themselves within a larger but closely-held story that I call the "personal narrative." This story is basically what we want (and desire) for ourselves "in a nutshell." It is the need for "deliverance" (again the desire to resume innocence), "salvation" (desire for security), emotional fulfillment (to lose control safely); for others to come after us and remember us, and to bond with a higher "element" that will save us from the terrors of the unknown, the worst of which is death (to transcend death). The personal narrative is often at the core of our emotional and sexual responses. These often intertwining responses become the material of both our spiritual feelings and our daily lives. In other words, they *are* what fulfill us. We see a certain bowdlerization of them in the commercial images that surround us: pop culture, advertising, and political slogans that basically boil down "ideas" to easily digested stupidities—these all utilize and prey on our needs to have our own *personal narratives* fulfilled.

Many of our desires stem from these narratives, and no matter how much we may try to repress them we do not actually escape far from them. So, in effect we are searching for these intensely important narratives that are actually already inside us. This means that when we do find them (or we are offered them on any level, whether in the pop world, or authentically, in real life), we react immediately and often positively. We jump at them, even if within this immediate reaction some fears are also ignited.

Often we find this happening in our approach to love, that is to immense, *genuine* connections that sometimes seem to have almost no "rational" basis for them. Why are we so crazy about this person? Why have we connected so deeply with him? What is it that is really drawing us to him? And what are the pitfalls involved with this connection—can we really trust him? Is this love returned?

The truth is that any real love connection is at the very core of ourselves—it is a continuous Deeper Self to Deeper Self connection, that sometimes does feel so immediate, so recognizable that the term "falling in love" is the only way you can describe it. You are "falling." It is unavoidable, and amazingly natural. It just seems to happen because your Deeper Self is open to it: the Deeper Self has recognized what is going on, sometimes even before you do on a conscious level—even though there may be external (that is social or material) aspects of both of you making this connection really difficult.

But a very deep personal narrative is being fulfilled, if not necessarily revealed—if only it were!—and this is what is drawing you so much to him, sometimes even without consciously knowing it. In what were classic heterosexual relationships, a constant *social* narrative was spread throughout the culture—and fed back to you so intensely, so often, that it was unavoidable. This caused generations of gay men (and often the women involved with them) to fall for it, too. It basically said that for every man there was a woman waiting, and vice versa. And that all you needed to do was find her (or *him*) to be happy.

We are still feeling this social narrative, although in reality it is no longer the case—as the divorce rate and the rate of unmarried people living either alone or together testify. But the current state of sexual intimacy has also spread an alternative "gay" narrative both to gay men as well as the rest of the culture. What I mean by this is that the "gay" narrative did not say that happiness was *inevitable*. But it could be reached with enough persistence and openness if you worked at it. So even the one girl for every guy and one guy for every girl model—the one based on inevitable "love and marriage"—is being questioned.

Does this mean that this "gay" narrative is being really normalized, reaching the rest of the population too, as straight couples wait longer to get married, as alternative forms of sexuality and relationships become more acceptable (and there will be more on that later in the chapter on bisexuality and polyamory), and as we see numbers of public figures whose own lives follow very diverse narratives that still work for them?

I believe it is, and for many younger people this is very true. Still, that social narrative of the waiting person, gay or not, is hard to deny.

I am not, to be perfectly honest, sure of the relationship between desire and a personal narrative—that is, where exactly does one lie inside another?—but I know that desire does illuminate and reveal, like a powerful light, our deeper narratives, just as these narratives, when understood, give definite conscious forms to desire. In other words, desire, as a large, emotionally-charged state, is the *truth* within us, but desire is found in many layers which are packaged or "housed" in symbols and metaphors that present the personal narrative to us.

46

The difficult thing is to identify these symbols and the desires within them, and, likewise, once exposed, to put these unmet desires which can be either so fulfilling or destructive, back into their metaphors or "houses" so that they can be dealt with, or at least more easily approached. You will see some of this happening in the chapters on BD/SM, various forms of "kink," and the extended discussions on spirituality.

13 Desire and Consciousness

"The truth is whatever proves itself to be good in the name of belief."

William James

As you can see, many of our desires come right out of consciousness, as it brings us these very important personal narratives, again "housing" the desire in a metaphor or symbol. As we learn to recognize something, we either desire it in some way, or try not to desire it—to avoid it—in other ways. We don't even want to think about it. We're scared of it. Many religious groups have a list of "forbidden" books, movies, ideas, and feelings that you, as a member, must reject to stay in the group, and "receive" God. The forbidden thing becomes in effect a symbol of everything that is evil and revolting to the group. Interestingly enough, in the period before the 1980s, that is, when irony came in full blast to popular culture, what was deemed detestable to the general population (in other words, the group Hollywood was trying to appeal to) was signaled immediately by titles involving Evil itself: "Flesh and the Devil," "The Devil Is a Woman," "A Touch of Evil," "Race with the Devil," and of course "The Devil and Miss Jones"—a fatal collision between the Lord of Darkness and a common lady.

(By the time "The Devil Wears Prada" came along, it was all a laugh—too much irony had come prancing into pop culture.)

A lot of this forbidden territory becomes a question of which "club" will you belong to? Will you belong to the Catholic club, the Jewish club, or the Islamic club? Will it be the straight club, which has its own handshake (firm to bone-crushing) and way of crossing the knee (manfully place ankle on opposing knee)? Or the gay one—which tells you how to dress and which singers to like? Or how about the bisexual club which everybody wants to belong to, but few want to admit belonging to?

There is also the black club, the white club, the "minority" club and the "majority" club, both of which are very hard to define at this point. And to make things more interesting, how about the Republican club, the Democratic club, the conservative or progressive club; the Right wing or the Left wing?

The important thing to these clubs is that you remain able and willing to shape your words and thoughts to remain a member in good standing. That you will *buy* into it, and even what you buy will represent your membership.

Since our buying is now seen as a reflection of other desires, consumerism has become an important gateway into many clubs, and sadly enough, has attempted to satisfy for many people the difficult but extremely important needs of their Deeper Self and deepest desires.

You may not become a really "bigger" person, but you can work like hell to afford to buy "bigger" things, ones that tip off your status. We now have a huge market in "luxury," even though the greatest luxury is still being yourself. But these "luxury" purchases have become instantly "readable" in our culture, as real interactions with people become less common. It is hard to see anyone anymore as they are hidden behind designer sunglasses, earphones, smart phones, tablets, and the other things one uses to keep themselves and others removed from a less predictable human environment.

One of my main feelings in this book is that by curbing desire, we also curb *consciousness*. I'm afraid this has become a big part of contemporary American life, and life all around the world. It has strangely enough led to another desire:

The desire to escape consciousness and avoid yourself. This is now a very operative desire for many people. Men, in an environment that is really designed to produce depression by depriving them of their most basic emotional and psychological needs (that is, for both genuine security *and* areas of personal freedom), operate on this desire all too often. We see it obviously enough in compulsive sex, alcohol, gambling, and drug addictions. But we don't even recognize it in obsessively following sports (which have become the universal, and safe, language of straight men and the gay men who want to emulate them). In exercise and body obsessions to the point of male anorexia (with some men seriously damaging themselves with products like human growth hormone); as well as other guys working themselves to death on the job, in order to escape their own anxieties and loneliness.

Consciousness, that is, *real* awareness, is scary. But until you have learned to make peace with the person you are and have established contact again with your own Deeper Self, avoiding it can be even more dangerous.

Other Important Desires Involving Consciousness

Desire for a life without fear. This is a deeper desire because it opens up in us a need to find a truly trustable partner—one whose openness to us, protectiveness, and goodness can transcend a lot of our feelings about "type," or even the more usual aspects of sexual attraction (that is, that someone looks a certain way or fulfills a certain role). A lot of men who go after a particular type of man repeatedly, one who appeals to them on a purely physical basis, cannot admit that what usually destroys these affairs, besides boredom, is basically a lack of trust: boredom and the lack of trust work smoothly together. Trust both requires and enables a deeper exchange of emotional energy, which recharges relationships and keeps them fresh. Trust also allows us to have the beautiful feeling that someone can actually see inside you to your own worth—regardless of the times you trip up, fuck up, or disappoint.

Once this trust has been experienced, then big barriers come down and amazing areas of sexual and emotional feelings open up.

Since to most outsiders these areas are usually hidden (and for important questions of privacy within a relationship they *should* be), the attraction of two men may seem a mystery. "What does he *really* see in *him*?"

What he sees is that he can trust his partner to understand him, and he can trust himself to be valued. And they can both trust themselves to go further into those important, fulfilling but sometimes scary territories we define as "love."

The desire for formality. This is a desire for the power *within* formality that formality genuinely contains. Many people, on face value, cannot understand this. They laugh at the idea of a total pacifist who gets a hard-on when a man in a military uniform approaches. The complete slacker hippy-dippy-type who secretly lusts for men in banker suits; or who throws over his lifestyle of pure slackerdom for a regular job. It's not simply financial security he wants; it's the sexual potential of power itself inside the suit. "Power," Henry Kissinger, the plain-looking right-hand-man to several presidents, once said, explaining his own attractiveness to gorgeous women, "is the world's most powerful aphrodisiac."

We now live in a time of bland, casual, inconsequential relationships that leave huge numbers of men and women hungry—in fact *ravenous*—for something else. They are tired of bowling alone. There is something about undoing a man's tie, unbuttoning his white shirt, and unhitching his belt that has more sexual energy than eons of stark-naked fuck parties.

I think a lot of people are starting to understand this.

The desire for informality. This is the opposite of the previous desire. What you want is a genuine, unbuttoned, stark naked intimacy with *yourself.* An intimacy that will protect and strengthen you, and bring others toward you.

Although masturbation can be a door to this, and may even be a part of it, it goes much deeper than the usual masturbatory fantasies, easily finding its way into those territories of spirituality I will talk about later.

Desire for a formality of intimacy. That is, an intimacy with definite boundaries around it, coming first from you and then from someone else. Desire can be an amazing, startling motor for this—suddenly you recognize your own intense feelings for someone else, but what is needed is a *formality* of intimacy to keep these feelings going: that there are genuine commitments here, or the intention of making them.

A formality of intimacy can foster monogamy, which, in itself, can give you, with the right man, huge emotional and sexual *freedom.* Within the privacy of this relationship there may be no bars at all, except ones of mutual respect and responsibility. This formality of intimacy can produce feelings of belonging and possession that you've always craved, but at the same time feared because of your own insecurities.

On the other hand, a *formality of intimacy* can also provide the framework for little or no commitment. This "formality" of intimacy was previously found in places like the baths, pre-AIDS, when men walked in, took their clothes off, wrapped a towel around themselves, and knew, sexually, what they were after—even if it often meant no more than a handshake afterwards. It is currently found in a multitude of queer (and now straight) hook-up sites, where people openly offer the most minimal amounts of themselves in order to "get off."

Usually the contract in these sites and venues is that this is a "sex only" situation, which has its pluses and minuses. But the main idea is: you are getting exactly what you bargained for, so don't ask for more. However, we all know that it is very human to do just that— "ask for more."

Desire for secrecy within intimacy. This is one of the most beautiful of all desires. Intimacy without *privacy* is impossible—one reason why genuine intimacy in our Post-Privacy Age is becoming harder and harder to achieve. In this era of solitary-confinement, office-cubicle isolation, as much as we want lots and lots of people—which can include your 2,000 Facebook friends—to unload on, genuine *intimacy* demands an environment of trust and privacy between two people.

(You can invite in a third person, but things can get strained.)

Men who are *good* at intimacy understand the importance of keeping trusts and secrets. There is a lot of power in being able to do both. This is not—under any circumstances—an invitation to violate the vulnerable: i.e., being privileged with so much information to show off how much power you now have. It's simply stating a fact.

The desire for privacy (especially in our world of loud cell phone calls, over-hyped social media saturation, and tabloid journalism) is a necessary part of intimacy. It can be used to aid the work of desire.

If fulfilling desires has been a difficult problem for you, then you should sincerely question the boundaries of privacy that you keep, and whom you have allowed within these boundaries.

14 Desire and Romanticism

"He was not like a man to her, he was an incarnation, a great phase of life. She saw him press the water out of his face and look at the bandage on his hand. And she knew it was all no good, and that she would never go beyond him, he was the final approximation of life to her."

D. H. Lawrence. *Women in Love.*

One of the harder things for many men to admit is their own desire for romance. There are of course romantic men and men who are self-described "romantics," but actually understanding (and admitting) the role and power of romance in their lives is difficult for most men. First of all, even defining "romance" is difficult, and the definition has certainly been robbed of its depth by the hold of women's romance novels and made-for-TV movies which adhere to fairly static, dumb formulas, usually involving two attractive men fighting over one helpless woman.

(OK, I admit, things have evolved. In more contemporary romance novels, the women are not always so helpless—but if they weren't helpless at all, they wouldn't be in the novel. Also, to complicate matters, we now have a thriving industry of gay men's romance novels, equipped with cardboard stock gay male characters aimed almost exclusively at a female market that enjoys the thrill of watching three guys in the throes of the same agony of choice women have long panted over.)

But to clear away the brambles, there are two excellent explanations of romance and romanticism that can be very helpful here. First, we'll go back to the French idea of *roman*, a novel or story; "romance" does involve a story. Second, we'll go back to the idea of "romantic" art, that is, art that involves a longing for something, as opposed to "classical" art (the "purified" art of the ancient Greeks), which is always self-contained. Therefore romantic love, and the desire for it, is about a longing for someone else, and it does contain a story: your own story. *When you can share your inner story with someone else—*and here we are talking about the real personal narrative—*the attachment becomes romantic*. Romantic attachments are filled with powerful emotional exchanges that can produce huge erotic energy between people. These "exchanges" include getting over loss, grief, set-backs, and other problems, as well as solving the basic human dilemma of aloneness, feeling insecure, and incomplete.

The main source of this energy is simple *recognition*: someone else can now recognize your story, can see you for what you are and "get" you.

These exchanges do not have to be sexual, that is, they can exist outside a sexual context leading up to orgasm. The sexuality in them can be extremely sublimated, as anyone can tell you who's been through a highly emotionally-charged spiritual or fraternal weekend retreat (such as a Masonic retreat, for instance), the kind where men feel so close to each other they can barely contain themselves. I will go into these experiences later in the desire for spirituality, but these kinds of extremely "touchy-feely" romantic "bro" experiences are common. For gay men involved with these experiences, they can be either frustrating or very much welcomed, depending upon their ability to put up with the frustration.

The big question in romantic love, the one that turns romance into the daily fiction of our lives, is who will submit to whom? We see this question constantly in TV dramas, sitcoms, romance novels, of course, and you will ask it in your own life when a romantic story of your own suddenly becomes . . . well, *real*.

Somebody "gets" you; he opens up this vast need you have not only to explain yourself—your actual Deeper Self—but to reveal it in a way that seems completely natural, totally organic to you. This is a huge human desire. And in deeply romantic love it *is* fulfilled but usually not without a lot of bumps along the way, because this kind of revelation makes you *very* vulnerable. You are stripping away many long-held defenses in order to come back to that state of exquisitely trusting, finally-offered innocence I spoke earlier about; an innocence that is also part of our most basic human desires.

Most people in the throes of romantic love do find that by opening up their own "story," they are also joining a larger one. As one close friend entrusted to me, "When I'm in love all love songs, even the silliest ones, make sense. They all talk directly to me."

You now understand the hidden messages in much of popular culture—which traditionally surfs on the explosive emotions of being in love. Being in love, which has definite hormonal and chemical components to it too, is like being on a rollercoaster of feelings, and romantic love is the front car you're in. It's carrying you through it: your whole "story" is opening up to another person, and welcoming him in. And it is at this point that the desire for romantic love meets the desire for spiritual love.

Thoughts for You

Have you ever been in love? What did it feel like?

_____

_____

_____

Are you still in love? If not, would you like to be in love?

_____

_____

_____

15 Desire and Spirituality, Furthering the Discussion

"So much of what we call 'spirituality' nowadays is just watered down romanticism."
Robert Musil, *The Man Without Qualities*, 1930

I spoke at some length about the spiritual connection to sexuality in the chapter on the imagination, but in this chapter I'll go one further—that is seeing *spirituality* within romanticism itself. It is very hard for many people to reconcile these very "twin" experiences of spirituality and desire: that is, that both involve the framework of a "story"—a deeper personal narrative—as well as *longing*, that is, the desire to be fulfilled by something other than yourself. By "yourself" I mean your basic aggressive drives, appetites, and needs. This longing is often incorporated into an idea of heaven, a longing for a return to holiness, purity, and innocence, bringing us back to that moment before consciousness delivered us to "evil" itself in the guise of too many temptations and wrong choices.

We want to formalize that state of innocence as it is recognized, or received from others, and partaken of. We do this through numerous rituals and ceremonies, that include many of the transitions of life (baptism, coming of age, engagement, marriage; even death as the transition back to heaven) as well as sexual rites involving releasing our everyday shell of the inhibitions which keep us away from those deeper experiences of union and love.

But first, to understand how desire fits into spirituality, and it does very much fit into it, you have to understand what religion and spirituality are, and that no matter how hard we may try to avoid either of them, it's almost impossible to. Why is this so?

It's because so much of what we call *religion* is simply embedded in the basic "hardware," or patterns, of human consciousness produced by the evolution of consciousness itself. Consciousness, in short, arose out of survival needs. In order to survive, the species that eventually became human had to leave the old instinctual patterns that doomed many other species to extinction. Awareness takes an individual outside *basic biological patterning*, even though this patterning is powerful, relieving most of the natural world of the exhaustive problems of decision-making it is incapable of performing. For instance if you have been biologically patterned as a species to migrate at a certain time of the year (when the sun is at a certain point on the horizon), you will do it—no matter what the actual temperature and wind patterns are.

If you do it enough times without taking into account conditions other than the sun's position on the horizon, you may be annihilated. But you won't worry about making the wrong decision. It was already been made for you, by biological patterning.

Awareness means that you *will* pay attention to the temperature in April and the wind patterns, and you will know that any decision you make will have to be based on many factors, some of which—in reality—may not be totally known to you. This leaves you to resorting to various alternatives in which humans have found solace (and some wisdom) for millennia. These include myths, stories, and the presence of wise men, seers, or magi. And also a strong evidence in nature of a more powerful, unseen Force than you, puny human that you are, are capable of being.

These "super-forces" come out of awareness's needs, because consciousness could only go so far before coming up against unforeseen events that were truly scary. We are talking about big ones, like storms, plagues, droughts, wars, famines, and of course the ultimate event, Death. Therefore consciousness itself tried to find its own "patterns," or *significances*, to consult, outside even our "normal" capacities of awareness.

Thus it was that the first humans starting to observe the world realized that just as in nature there was a hierarchy of predators in the "food chain," in their own lives there was a hierarchy as well. Something was above *them* in the chain and it was fairly logical to locate this higher element in the heavens, where the most powerful forces of weather originated, and the constellations themselves stood as reminders of eternal mysteries.

But this very strong "something," and the forces behind it, needed to have names. It needed to have faces, respect, and—of this these humans were convinced—this "something" wanted in turn to locate "friends" or allies, below.

This friendship, or "special" relationship to the God-forces, resulted in great power. We see that even today, as our own contemporary level of anxiety, brought on by even more awareness and hyper-consciousness, has shot straight up. This seems a paradox: We think of hyper-religious periods as being in the Dark Ages, when galloping fear and ignorance brought on religious hysteria. Yet we are living in a very religious period, brought on by anxieties born of our 24/7 levels of consciousness: we have "too much information" and need to escape it—or, at least make peace with its limitations—for something else.

So religion, in one form or another, is still here with us. But even if religion were shorn of all its power (which can become quite perverse, as religious leaders are summoned to influence political decisions completely outside their actual range of knowledge), religious feelings would still have meaning in the lives of human beings.

Why?

First, because as much as we may try to evade the weight and burdens of everyday awareness—all those bills to pay, problems at work, friends who disappoint us, absence, grieving, and death—there is an inner and more universal Consciousness that is conveyed to us through three very important channels. They are art, religion, and sex, and they are capable of delivering a huge support to our lives, when awareness itself simply becomes too much of a burden. This universal Consciousness is also very much bound up within the "Deeper Self," that inner "gyro" that keeps us balanced.

Religion strives to bring us closer to this; sex and art can open us up to it as well, if both sex and art are engaged in a positive, humane, and nurturing way.

Secondly, religion satisfies the need for that personal narrative all human beings have that I have talked about, that story of your life written *larger* than you are, but with you still in it. The personal narrative attempts to answer the primary questions we all ask, such as: Where did I come from? How did I become the person I am? How will I get along in the world—with others and myself? What will give me the most happiness by myself, and still satisfy the deep needs I have for closeness with others?

And of course, again the final question: How will I prepare myself, emotionally, psychologically, and spiritually, for my own death?

This personal narrative is laid out for us by endlessly retold stories, parables, myths, and also by rules. In religion, it is also accompanied by promises ("covenants,") stating that those who believe in the myths—and obey the rules—will reap rewards, either now or in the Hereafter. In the past, the most obvious reward was in material benefits. God promised the ancient Hebrews ("the Children of Israel"), that they would prosper under his guidance, becoming as plentiful as the stars in the heavens, or the grains of sand by the sea. But the other, more powerful reward would be found in the acceptance and implantation of a framework of morality which crude human activity alone, guided merely by "instincts" (another word for self-interests) would either trample upon or destroy.

This morality usually went beyond the "golden rule."

For the ancient Hebrews and their spiritual descendants among Christians and Moslems, it presented a complex series of restrictions on behavior, diet, and even marriage and associations which would in effect be punishing and limiting, but which also offered the defining boundaries of a community itself: one that would no longer rely simply on racial characteristics or political borders. This meant you could be a part of a community and physically leave it, and still carry the moral code of your community with you. To many people today, this is still a huge attraction of religion—that a moral code binds them to goodness beyond their ability to understand it.

A condition of carrying the moral code, though, was, again, always being under the burdens of consciousness or *awareness*. You knew you had to stay within the code to belong, and it was not going to be easy be-cause of the far-reaching effects of the code. The code made you aware of being different, certainly different from those people who did not obey it. Being different presented a genuine conflict for many people.

The conflict was that you were now trying hard to be outside the very Nature that spawned you: the nature of sex (and of birth) itself that ties us to our animal roots. This means that the moral code, no matter how noble its intentions, pulls us away from our own *innate* "natures," into a more artificial *space*, even if it is a space that connects us to people with whom we may have that close relationship based on shared beliefs and even kinships. I refer to this close relationship as a "reli-gious intimacy." For many people, this is one of the great intimacies of their lives, and it is very hard to live without it.

Religious Intimacy vs. Self-Intimacy

What this means is that although there is, within an often very sup-portive communal space, this "religious" intimacy important to many people, they are also sacrificing a vital *self-intimacy* within the same space, the loss of which can be both psychologically painful and costly (a fact seen in the rate of alcoholism among, for example, celibate priests and nuns). Unfortunately, due to the indoctrination they receive, many religious people are not even aware of the source of this psychological pain. Something is missing, but they cannot even question why. But to make up for this loss, many religious gay men from orthodox or fundamentalist backgrounds strive to become even *more* religious, more punitive and restrictive in their approach both to themselves and others. We see this situation happening in a repressive Catholic hierarchy that has veered so far to the exclusion of gays and lesbians that the rank-and-file of the faithful in America no longer adheres to it, in an Orthodox Jewish homophobia bordering on hysteria, and in more recent violent Moslem reactions to homosexuality (when classically Islam was more tolerant) to name only a very few examples—there are many more.

In these hyper-religious examples any form of genuine *self-intimacy* is shoved aside (under the usual admonishments of avoidances of "selfishness" or "sin") in the pursuit of an even more intense religious intimacy that, in itself, easily mimics sadomasochism.

In these situations, the most difficult sacrifice—but the ones with the biggest "pay out"—is to have whatever constitutes your own real *self* replaced by a religious substitute that can be very powerful, because you are sure *it* is now following your own *personal narrative*. This means that you will, at some point, join a "welcoming" but totally desexualized God-force and completely offer yourself to it, while withholding any (if not all) of the deeper, primal sexual instincts you have.

In this manner, any residual *self-intimacy* that remains becomes completely "spiritualized."

This particular personal narrative is found in the total submission of priests and spiritual brothers to a religious superior (which often has more than a *surface* sado-masochistic element in it, to the full satisfaction of both parties: those submitting and those above them). It is also frequently found in the seemingly amazing joy of trying to obliterate your ego in order to do "good work," an experience witnessed by men who go out on missionary quests to "help the natives," while at the same time repressing any sexual interest in them. And it is found in other forms of submission, like men who destroy themselves overworking for professional reasons, or who over-train and exercise, or renounce all worldly rewards or comfort for a "just" cause that may be, in fact, very indifferent to them.

Masturbation

It is difficult to talk about "self-intimacy" without even a wink at masturbation, which Judeo-Christianity thoroughly rejected as a "waste" or spilling of sperm (or, in the female as a rejection of "natural" male advances), but which most men understand as a practice that allows them a chance for much needed private time and activity. For many men masturbation is as close to an act of intense ego-releasing meditation as they will get. In Victorian times the code word for masturbation was "reverie;" men would casually ask one another if they ever "enjoyed reverie." (Mutual masturbation, by the way, was not considered sex at all, but a form of intense friendship sharing.) "Reverie" was often associated with book reading, since books were expensive and a private indulgence, as opposed to newspapers, a form of mass communication. So men who read books, especially books of poetry or novels, were often seen as suspect of masturbating.

Masturbation, aside from invoking sexual fantasies (or even resulting from sexual fantasies) also invoked spiritual ones: that is, fantasies of incorporating yourself with a higher force, such as a more powerful man, and of being delivered from the daily grind of life to another more fantastical existence, even if only after death.

I am not saying here that all of Christianity may be based on shared, covert masturbation fantasies, but the fact that sexuality among men was so condemned by Judaic (or Levitical) law has often made me wonder if the Essene cults which were examples of intense (and, easily romantic) male bonding, that became so secretive and underground during the Roman occupation of Palestine, could have led to an environment in which fervent messianic and sexual feelings gave way to . . . well, . . . this has caused more than one person to suggest that these feelings eventually fleshed themselves into the persons we now may (or can) associate with the cult of Jesus, who was often called the "lover of our souls."

I will talk more about "reverie" in other chapters in this book, but the relationship between desire as a feeling that connects us to others and to ourselves, and to the private engagement in secret thoughts— "reverie"—is only too obvious. I will also be talking about the important experience I refer to as "self love" later on; and of course I hope that you'll start thinking about your own closely-held "reveries" at various points in this book.

The Soul

This leads us to the appearance of the soul, the incarnation of the Spirit itself, and how this amazing psychological/spiritual concept is also involved with desire.

First it is important to understand what is meant by the phenomenon of the soul and how it came about. The idea of a "soul" first appeared to the ancient Egyptians who, in an example of genuine spiritual "genius," were able to split the human persona into various components. There was of course the gross or material body, which normally would not survive death, unless something very special was done to it, which they learned how to do and perfected as a sacred art form. Then there was the idea of the "shadow," or the personality behind the body—that aspect which we often speak of now as the "darker" side, the side that understands guilt and sin. Then there was the idea of the soul, the *ka*, which would survive death and go on its own journey to the Underworld where it would be judged by Osiris, the Egyptian god of rebirth, who would weigh the *ka* in the form of the deceased's heart on a scale that had to be balanced by the feather of truth. To the Egyptians, the heart and the soul were inextricably bound together, and we still speak of "heart and soul" as being our own powerful indicators of sincerity and truthfulness.

The expressions, myths, and rituals gathered around Osiris, the ancient god of rebirth and resurrection, also uncannily prefigure Christian ideas, so that ancient Egyptians also considered themselves personally "reborn" in Osiris, and referred to him as "the lover of my soul"—in that Osiris would identity—and claim—your very essence, the most vulnerable part of you that held all of your most private feelings, needs, and desires.

If you look, though, directly at the concept of the soul, you will see in it a beautiful refinement of consciousness. Namely the soul is not actually "conscious" of anything, but capable of representing very neatly a higher level of the imagination, which will readily (and "innocently," i.e., without questions) contain the deeper personal narratives for which humans long. The deepest and most personal of these narratives (and let's get down to basics here: "narrative" is simply another name for story) is one that reaches out toward and is satisfied, on its deepest level, by *love*.

Love is hugely satisfying and necessary for humans, despite all of our too common cynicism regarding it. Although diamonds are still "a girl's best friend," they don't keep you warm at night, and no one looks forward to dying with only those "rocks" as their company.

But in reaching out toward love (and let's face it: we all do that), people deliver themselves into a terrible, frightening state of vulnerability. Love, by definition, is the attraction to someone outside yourself, but as you approach it you have to surrender very important and strategic parts of yourself—namely, your own *defenses*.

Spiritualized Desires

Here is where spirituality (namely, a recognition of the "Spirit," the soul, as a part of the human persona) and *desire* do run on the same track, because imbuing something with a "spiritual love" can offer you a state of "being in love" without the jealousy, possessiveness, and usual range of problems and insecurities that physical (or "coupled") love at some point almost inevitably presents.

For centuries, in strongly enforced heterosexual relationships, child production as a goal kept these insecurities at bay: By having children, a couple opened themselves up to other experiences and feelings. In other words, having children (i.e., procreating) became a "sacrament" in itself. It was a *sacrifice* to have children, but it led to other spiritual benefits—ones which most people could not imagine having by themselves, especially since heterosexual love (in the case of marriage) was so rigidly enforced. You might not truly love your spouse but you would certainly love your children, or the family entity that now shielded you from the problems of loneliness and old age.

"Spirituality," then, was engaged to entwine carnal desires and legitimize them with the responsibilities of caring, nurturing, protecting, and (often with some direct enforcement by social codes) even loving another person. This also diffused *desire*, so that what was once considered dirty, "selfish," or obscene (the demands of a naked sexual appetite) could still hang around as a source of energy behind that state of the emotionally-charged "exaltation" which religion offers.

(Some might say that this "exaltation" is simply an inflated sense of self—lower case "self"—but, certainly, in a lot of cases I've seen, that's not so bad either.)

Compared to the dangers of physicalized *desire* (those old "appetites" again) acting solely on its own, *spiritualized* desire offers amazingly safe protections from many "issues," problems, and feelings. There is not simply the hypocrisy that you can desire God and *still* desire boys, but the security offered in the feeling that if you desire God *enough*, the desire for boys will disappear.

(Or, the converse feeling: that you can even be permitted the desire for *boys*, if *only* you desire God enough.)

In our own time, we have a proliferation of "12-Step" programs that run along the same track. You offer up to a "higher force" your problems with alcohol, drugs, gambling, shopping, or even sex-addiction. And you join a working community of people who have done the same thing.

What this brings about is an intense opening of feelings among co-spiritualists. All of your most vulnerable, secretive aspects can now be channeled through a new "sacred" narrative that may feel extremely personal to you, but in some of its exquisitely essential Mystery, shared by others in your company also. The compassion and agonies of Christ, the renunciations and asceticism of the Buddha, the revelations and sacrifices of Abraham, the powers and perceptions of Mohammed, are now all part of your own *personal narrative*, shielding your own most secret desires and permitting them, against all prohibitions, even to exist, without destroying you.

In the "old days," when sex was extremely forbidden to talk about except in terms of either marriage or hell-fire, many queer men found refuge in the church, whether it was Catholicism, High Church Episcopalianism, or even some of the more hard-shell branches of Protestantism where these men found themselves working as organists or choir masters. What it meant was these men were shielded from their unquestionable obligations to be husbands, or "normal," regular-guy back-slapping sportsmen, although many of them could still masquerade as that if necessary. We still see this kind of masquerade going on today when fundamentalists preachers are caught in public restrooms or with paid male escorts, even while still desperately trying to deny any wrong doing.

What is important for you to understand as you approach, honestly, your own desires, through the gateway of a personal narrative, is that it is no sin or problem to share desire with spirituality, as long as others are not being victimized in the process. This is where going into this with your eyes open and your feelings out is very important. But you should have some defenses, too, that come from your own Deeper Self, because mixing desire and the Spirit can also expose a lot of vulnerability, as so many members of cults, with their own charismatic manipulative leaders, have found out.

In these cases, you feel totally betrayed: you have not only offered up (and sometimes not even willingly) your body, but also your soul to this person who is now acting in the role of "God's messenger," and he has taken it and simply defiled it. Men who have been involved in these situations often end up doubly hurt: their faith in themselves is destroyed, as well as their faith in Faith. This can lead to a damaging, if not dangerous emotional shutting down, leading to suicide. So it's important to understand that twinning desire and spirituality requires some fences around it within your own heart.

Thoughts for You

Have you ever had a spiritual moment that was also warmed with intense desire? Can you speak of it?

_____

_____

_____

16 What You Should Know About 9 Secret and Very Powerful Personal Narratives

"Human behavior flows from three main sources: desire, emotion, and knowledge."

Plato

If the essence of religion is a personal narrative and I believe it is, in the form of "belief," that is a personal approach to, or a revelation of, a higher Force, then within these personal narratives are deeper and even more secret stories, ones that reveal even more personal elements of us. Here are a nine of these deeper stories—you may actually have one of your own—that will become very useful to us in the next discussion.

The stranger as angel. One of the most beautiful of all spiritual narratives, it reveals the innocence we want to find, explore and plumb, and also the idea that even the most "anonymous" or *unexpected* of personal (or sexual) encounters can have a genuine element of meaning and purpose to them. One of the hallmarks of angels is that they are directed by God, and are unimpeded by the conflicts of human consciousness (except of course in the event of rebellious angels, such as Lucifer, the bringer of light). What this means, in the field of desire, is that someone can come into your life with a strictly *sexual* purpose or message and still bring to you a divine *mission* in that purpose or message.

What is the message? An amazing revelation of self—simple as that.

Here clothes, fronts, façades, and bullshit are dropped, and in this momentary exchange of personalities, something real and *angelic* happens. Men who have tried hallucinogenic drugs in very sexualized environments, such as bathhouses, sex clubs, or orgies, often report that they have experienced this narrative. They are attracted to a man for his personal beauty, but also realize that within both this attraction and him, is a powerful fulfilling innocence and truthfulness. Sometimes this is purely part of the hallucinogenic properties of drugs, but there is also

66

an aspect that the hallucinogens may have opened up sacred feelings of intense intimacy that were previously repressed.

This leads me to feel that there can be something very seductive about this secret narrative, and, sometimes, dangerously so: a very beautiful angel can also lead you in his "innocence" to real drug abuse, and/or a level of "intimacy" that is not only unreal, but can be manipulative and deadly. In other words, some sweet and exciting stranger can also lead you to your own destruction. So, in accepting the "stranger as angel," it is important to keep both eyes open.

Although I feel that the "stranger as angel" spiritual narrative works beautifully in gay sexual settings, it is universal. Men who previously only acted heterosexually may find themselves drawn to a man because of this narrative, thereby being pulled into bisexual feelings. Men seek the "angelic" in women, and one of the sadder aspects of the "double standard" is that when women fall off the "angel" pedestal, the fall is disastrous. When gay men encounter this angel aspect in another man, it is emotionally disarming; when insecure straight men do it, it is infuriating and even disgusting to them, as seen in Herman Melville's long short story "Billy Budd," when a handsome sailor's beautiful purity of heart leads to his tragedy.

The lost twin or brother who has a psychic history with you. A very powerful, narrative, it identifies a sexual experience as having an almost unfathomable connection with you—that is, one that bonds itself to you on a psychic (and even biological) level, as a renewed connection with a blood relative might have. For men, the brother connection is extremely deep, and also often conflicted. We have intense sibling rivalries as well as intense sibling bonding. So this deeper narrative opens up amazing vistas of connection: the idea that you have connected with another man in a way that cannot be sundered even by the usual male flashes of temper from arguments, conflicts of opinions, or *macho* competition. You are brothers who are now united, and that relationship has been set.

Although women may easily refer to themselves as "sisters," for men to refer to themselves as *brothers* takes a much stronger effort and expenditure of tightly held emotional currency: it means a real commitment and, as anyone who's ever been initiated into a fraternity knows, these commitments are unfathomably deep. The brother narrative can also spiritualize and sexualize certain job relationships, men whose professions are extremely stressful or dangerous, such as firemen, policemen, men in the armed forces, medics, and men separated from their normal environments, out there together doing special "men's," or dangerous, work all on their own.

Therefore this deeper brother narrative fuels a great number of almost universal sexual fantasies: the hot cops, firemen, and soldiers who facing a wall of danger, will make themselves available to our own pent-up feelings. The sexualized "brother" narrative can also add a powerful charge to a gay marriage rite; that is, that a man has a role in your life beyond the normal limitations of sexual interest, or the regular tides of personal problems that wash over and can wash out any marriage. He is now the deepest part of your family: a brother under the skin and in the heart.

The wounded soldier waiting to be healed. In the jungle of male encounters where men casually expose so little of themselves, to find yourself in a place of vulnerability and then to offer your wounds to another man is an act of enormous trust. Trust is a profoundly erotic bonding element between men, that unfortunately is often not found in many standard male-female couplings which rely, generally, on simple biological patterning to work. (The truthfulness of this is again found in the "double standard": men are expected to cheat on their wives, but women must never cheat on their husbands. To do so can be fatal for women. Therefore throughout history, men did not trust women, and women were not allowed even to think about actually trusting their husbands: this was simply not part of the "double standard." It has resulted in the famous, and stupidly juvenile dictum "bro's before ho's".)

So when men cast aside their natural wariness towards other men, and offer their vulnerabilities to them, huge emotional reserves are opened as well. For some straight men, this can be extremely upsetting, resulting in homophobic violence. The terrible thing is that many straight men actually go after these situations (as in the famous "Boy, was I drunk last night!" defense) in order to first release a lot of pent-up feelings, enjoy them, and then in cold daylight, resort to violence.

The healer looking for release. The male healer is in the "feminine" role of nurturer, and for many men this provokes role anxiety by going against the staunchly masculine role of Defender of Power. This role anxiety is dispelled in the crucial, even "magical" moment when healing actually takes place. At that point, great reserves of feeling can be exposed on the part of both the healed and the *healer*, so that the healer finds release from his own problems by engaging with another man (or woman) with tenderness, vulnerability, and caring. He is now, in effect, in the priest role, and for thousands of years the priest and physician were seen in the same person: both roles relied on "magic," that is a belief in the unexplainable. Many religious celebrations or rituals are actually veiled healings: Easter, celebrating the healing release of Christ from death; Passover, celebrating "healing" from slavery; and Rosh Hashanah (Jewish New Year), celebrating the healing pardon of Abraham from the sacrifice of Isaac.

Men who are in a "top" role in leather/S&M play are also these healers looking for release. They are providing a magical or facilitated environment for other men—as are women who are also tops. They are also "healing" the gulf—the open wounds—between intense feelings and unmet needs, using the doors of desire to get to them.

A sacrifice of freedom in order to gain transcendent insight or emotional release. In this narrative, freedom is seen as the tyranny of too many choices and too many ambushing temptations—all amounting, after a lot of effort, to *nothing*. Freedom, then, is open to doubt, but its excesses can be tamed through discipline, seen as a sacrifice of comfort, imposed either from within or outside yourself.

This sacrifice may come after an internal struggle that, in itself, may be extremely sexual, because it involves a lot of pent-up erotic energy. We find this narrative in many religious rituals of submission (as in the Catholic priestly submission to authority—"poverty, chastity, and obedience"—which I have spoken about earlier), and of course in S&M rituals in which the struggle to maintain discipline can also be charged with sexual heat and electricity.

This secret narrative also brings many men back to a school boy story of being punished by someone in power, and then rewarded by this person's love: "Daddy" or the "Master" after imposing a strict discipline, is now loving his "boy," binding the two of them in an intense very cathartic, and "hot," secret harmony.

Releasing the curious, hungering child within. As in "the stranger as angel," this is one of those bedrock narratives. It appeals directly to a need to revert to our own innocence and purity, after the daily hard-grinding cynicism of "normal" life. The child may be within you, or you may encourage it in another person and then share these feelings of renewal. It may take some excavation to get to this narrative, although people who have been using narratives for a long time, either through therapy or sexual ritual, easily experience it. The important thing within this narrative is being emotionally (and sexually) nourished, but there is also a willingness to dispense with filters, or defenses, which means that the narrative can only take place in an environment of genuine *trust*.

Many men come to this secret narrative through spiritual doors, seeing themselves as one of God's children, seeking guidance and warmth. This gives other men in religious environments, as I have said, huge power over them—which can be easily abused. But when taken into sexual places, this secret narrative can be immensely fulfilling.

The powerful, nurturing father. Like the Emperor card in the Tarot, the father narrative represents not simply the father as maintainer of discipline, but the father as protector, healer, and guardian of structure. He has an inner nature that is warmly nourishing (in fact merging with feminine), but an exterior providing the protection that allows for deeper trust. In American society, formed in a crucible of constant frontier danger, the father or "Daddy" image is immensely powerful. We may want Daddy to double as the Brother, but not *too* much—in this secret narrative he must be that final, powerful bulwark of a protecting structure. Therefore the nurturing father narrative upholds a gender *polarity* that, despite many people's strong feelings about sexism and the fight against it, is still immensely, powerfully attractive.

There is a search here also for God, who is seen as our Father, but what makes the father eminently appealing is on one hand his approachability—that we can seek his attention—and on the other, his own almost impenetrable defenses: he does represent a stunning solidity of *power*—one that can confront our fears and dangers, real or psychic, and dispel them. The father narrative doubles back into the desire for formality: for roles and boundaries, and the comfort in sexually accepting them.

A note about gender polarity: In our age of gender fluidity, sexual or gender polarity is extremely charged. Even admitting that you find gender polarities exciting on a fantasy level is disquieting or even disgusting to some people. However, as I will talk about later in the chapter on BD/SM, down in these deep, bedrock personal narratives, there are primal feelings way past political correctness—and many of these feelings flow toward these basic polarities of male or female (or the characteristics of maleness and femaleness), and find huge expression in them.

The narrative of change or Metamorphosis. Turning into a stranger, turning into an angel, turning into a Daddy, turning into a child—the point of metamorphosis in a secret narrative is both exciting as it can be also unsettling, falling into our own worst Jekyll-and-Hyde fears. Nightmares are filled with metamorphoses (humans turning to monsters; familiar people turning to thugs or worse), but so are our desires and wishes. We wish to be hugely successful, powerful, and rich. We wish to become sexually not only fulfilled but even rampantly desirable. Metamorphosis can inflate you to a point that you no longer recognize yourself—an intense fantasy for some people: that you are now "new" even to yourself—but it can come with a terrible price: That you have alienated those whose love means everything to you. Since sex is often very much a "trip," this secret narrative presents places where you actually change into another personality: one freer, wilder maybe. Certainly unbothered by old inhibitions and anxieties.

The real challenge though is finding some Father, some Guide who will help you through the changes, to make sure you don't go completely "overboard."

Narratives of activities. Flying, swimming, wrestling, boxing, sleeping, urinating, becoming naked, being seduced in our sleep or sexually aroused in an unconventional place. Being constrained, tied down, chained, or unchained. Released. Moving, packing, sharing items, fluids, or tokens of meaning. Eating, cooking, feeding or being fed—these are only some of the narratives of activities that lend themselves to secret meanings in our lives. In many of these activities, energy is being compressed and then re-directed toward release, producing what I call a "fissionable" moment: that is, extremely emotionally powerful. The sexual implications of these activities are obvious, but often the emotional connections to our deeper narratives are not. The narratives of activities suggest working "cures" to many of our problems, such as feeling inadequate, small, shameful, weak, powerless; psychologically as well as physically hungry; in pain, or painfully alone. Therefore, turning any aspect of these narratives of activities into sexual experiences can be extremely satisfying.

Important Work for You

Do you have a particular attachment or association to one of these narratives you need to think about?

_____

_____

_____

Do one of these narratives really bother you? Can you discuss why this is so?

_____

_____

_____

CHAPTER 17

Our Connections to Deeper Personal Narratives and Fictions

"I got a sleeping-suit out of my room and, coming back on deck, saw the naked man from the sea sitting on the main-hatch, glimmering white in the darkness, his elbows on his knees and his head in his hands. In a moment he had concealed his damp body in a sleeping-suit of the same grey-stripe pattern as the one I was wearing and followed me like my double on the poop. Together we moved right aft, barefooted, silent."

Joseph Conrad, "The Secret Sharer."

Great fictions, that is the stories that authentically appeal to us, that grip and hold us, are colored with deeper personal narratives, some of them directly on the surface of the story, others like deep water explorers, diving under the story itself, so that the story then becomes open to our desires. An interesting phenomenon is the closeness of gay men to stories, perhaps because for so long most of us could not tell our own story out loud. So we clung to stories and saw our own story in them. Whether the story was in a movie from the Golden Age of Hollywood, such as *The Wizard of Oz* or *All About Eve*, or a classic novel, the important thing was that we saw our own lives in it taking form.

A perfect example of this is Joseph Conrad's long short story "The Secret Sharer," about a young ship captain who on his first commissioned voyage out into open water pulls a handsome young sailor from another ship, naked out of the sea. It turns out that the sailor has committed a crime, killing a crewmember on his ship, who was insolent to him during a violent storm. The young captain takes pity on this sailor and identifies with him, so that he slips the man into his own extremely close captain's quarters, and hides him from his crew. Conrad's descriptions of the incredible intimacy of the two men, both bound by their feelings of being different and alienated from others around them, verges on the overtly sexual without ever going there: in Conrad's time, this would have been impossible. At the end of the story, the young captain is able to steer his boat close enough to approaching land for the sailor to jump overboard and survive, and his boat is saved from crashing on the rocks by the young captain's own skills as a seaman.

"The Secret Sharer" came out in 1910, and for more than a century gay men have read into it an erotic subtext that Conrad and his critics have always denied. It is easy to see, though, several deeper personal narratives within the story: the lost twin or brother, the wounded soldier waiting to be healed, or the healer waiting to be released. Whether it is done consciously or unconsciously, locating these narratives within fictions gives the stories huge emotional depth and connections to us. It also reveals a point of desire in the story that in the past would have been solidly repressed. Repressed even to the point of violence.

Another example of this is the famous nude wrestling scene between the sensitive Rupert Birkin and the impulsive Gerald Crich in D. H. Lawrence's masterpiece *Women in Love*, from 1920. Here two men are so combustively connected to each other that all they can do is fight. It is a white-hot deeper narrative of activity: wrestling becomes a substitute for sex (although in many potent sexual fetishes, it can be a prelude). Another deeper narrative is the relationship of anger to sexuality: that is, that anger can also unmask deeper feelings of genuine emotional and sexual surrender.

In a coming chapter on "Your Own Greenwood of Desire," I talk about what "good" girls really want and what "bad" boys want, but suffice it to say that sometimes it requires a choreographed explosion to break the ice for both.

18 *[Bingo!]* Spiritual Consummation

"Urshanabi guided the ecstatic man away
to the other shore, and when they parted
Gilgamesh was alone again, but not
with loneliness or the memory of death."
Gilgamesh, translated by Herbert Mason.

When these deeper secret narratives are allowed to—or even invited to—take part in a sexual script, then what takes place is what I call "spiritual consummation." Sometimes in spiritual consummation, the sexual script may be extremely covert: there is such an intensity of connection that the usual erotic play may seem too crude, threatening, obvious, or clumsy ("gross") to enter into the picture. No matter, the level of intimacy is still shattering. You are not the person you were before it happened. Spiritual consummation can take place in a purely religious setting (and has for thousands of years); it can take place during one of those Black Nights of the Soul, as the Irish call them, usually facilitated by a lot of drinking; or at a moment of intense emotional jeopardy when healing and the person offering you healing take on huge significance in your life.

Sometimes, then, this form of spiritual consummation can be extended into a longer viable relationship, but there is usually a safety valve of withdrawal that takes place afterwards. In other words, even after a relatively long-term experience of it, say, several days or a week, you and your co-adventurers will discover a need to return to what might be called "normal life." That is eating, sleeping, thinking, working, doing the dishes, pissing and using the bathroom, without any quotation marks around them. Still this sense of being connected on a level that is anything but "normal" is phenomenal, in fact life changing.

(In my previous book *How to Survive Your Own Gay Life*, Belhue Press, 1999, I laid out the concept that "Intimacy is finite." In other words, we need to recharge after it. So, no matter what your investments in love and intimacy are, there is a normal need to return to some form of everyday life in all of us.)

Spiritual consummation and war go together incredibly well, and many ancient people understood the close relationship between states of war and sexuality. War, in other words, is caused by jealousy, envy, spite, arrogance, and resentment, feelings often engrained in sexual situations. War is also "cured," or healed, by a return to innocence, by the empowerment or recognition of the "Father," and by a return to a state of calm and fulfillment: truly that of post-orgasm. On the other hand, war is very much a theatrical format—it involves rehearsals, staging areas, and an arrangement of forces that to any visitor from Outer Space would seem completely in line, say, for a production of *West Side Story*. Spiritual consummation though is the opposite of this: while it is taking place it seems so utterly natural that it's difficult not to question why the whole world is not involved with it, which leads us to—

A Simple Question

Why isn't the world experiencing spiritual consummation all the time? And, another question: how much of what we call "religion" has been derived from it?

Are the ecstatic states of religion simply moments of spiritual consummation *deprived*—because of shame—of a sexual context? In what used to be called "pagan" worship, which revered Nature and the natural world, sexual ecstasy was encouraged and not repressed. After Christianity, with its background of monotheism and Levitical law, triumphed in the West, sex was relegated to the Devil's playground, and feelings of ecstatic pleasure and fulfillment could only be deemed acceptable as the result of extreme deprivation. The immediate followers of Jesus, after extended periods of fasting and celibacy, were expected to have and even encouraged to have intense religious experiences, i.e., visions. As long as these visions were of course acceptable by the standards of the early church.

Research has recently revealed that the early church, up to about 400 CE, was not so condemning of homosexuality and bisexuality as the later church was, after Christianity became the dominant force in the Western world. (Despite the fact that in parts of rural Eastern Europe, evidences of paganism continued until as late as the Reformation, resulting in virulent campaigns of suppression and genocide.) One of my own feelings, which many gay liberationists share, is that the early followers of Jesus contained a large number of men and women drawn to their own sex and to romantic same-sex attachments. The fact that Jesus's message was steeped in love for one's fellow person, for strangers, for the vulnerable, and poor—a message absolutely ignored by much of later Christianity—appealed directly to queer Hebrews of Greco-Roman Palestine, who might have found some refuge in Roman paganism, but who could not, on any grounds, desert their Hebraic roots to embrace those already established pagan attitudes of what now might be termed "multi-culturalism."

So to answer the questions: Why isn't the world experiencing spiritual consummation all the time? There is a huge amount of fear around this, as well as a repression about identifying it.

And, yes, a lot of religious feelings are involved with it.

Approaching Spiritual Consummation

How do you accept, encourage, and invite spiritual consummation?

First, by laying a groundwork of mutual trust between you and your partner. People often feel that trust is based on complete acceptance. Not true. You don't have to accept everything about a partner, to do so in fact could put you in a situation of real emotional blackmail and resentment. But you do have to accept a groundwork that allows honesty on both sides. In other words, the same groundwork that encourages you to be as sensitive to his feelings as you want him to be sensitive to yours.

"Your feelings are very important to me." Learn to say that, and mean it.

Talk about your own deeper narratives, but, even more important, feel that even the ones you cannot talk about are being honored by the two of you.

"Tell me what you would like me to do, and what you want to do."

Provide a space and time that is as sacred sexually as it is spiritually. Realize that this kind of sexuality is not about acts as it is about attitudes: establish a reverence for each other, and for the time you are together and the place you are together. Realize that things will heat up not just because the sex is so good, but because of the revelations of where the sex is coming from: your own deepest feelings, history, *desires* of course, and the hidden personal narratives behind them.

Do not close off parts of your imagination—in fact, invite them. For some men, used to dealing with the world on what is now might be termed a constant "politically correct" basis (in other words, telling people what you're sure they need to hear), inviting in these closed off parts of the imagination can be either threatening, or intensely liberating. But, recognize, also, in this sensitivity you are showing toward someone else, having some definite boundaries are good. So, if you (or your partner) have areas of great sensitivity, explore them carefully. An example is you may want to explore bondage, either being tied up or tying him up. This practice may remind him of a horrible humiliation he had as a kid—so don't insist on it and tread very carefully around the suggestion of it.

Questions

Have you experienced "spiritual consummation" before without knowing it?

What did it feel like? How long did it last? Would you like to repeat the experience?

Your answers:

_____

_____

_____

19 A Very Important Practice: Sex as Worship

"Love is simply the name for the desire and pursuit of the whole."

Plato, *The Symposium*

This leads us to one of the most significant practices of the manly pursuit of desire and love: seeing sexuality as another form of worship. One thing is certain: it's not new. In the days before Christian Puritan repression came in, many cultures revered sex as a form of worship not only to the gods and goddesses who resided over sex, but also as a form of nature worship itself. Just as sex is natural in nature, sex also has a natural role in honoring nature, both the natural world's beauty and complexity as well as our own human nature and a fuller experience of it. Therefore realize that in bringing your partner into your mouth, you are bringing in the entire earth and the sky, too. That he has now become the body of God, offering you this sacrament, just as you, too, have become the agent of God, partaking in it; and in revering and loving one another's body, you are extending this love and the consciousness that goes with it, to the Universe.

With this in mind, sex can become extended to last for hours, even for days, because it does not simply end in orgasm, but ends only when you revert back to the regular consciousness of life: i.e., the regular, everyday tasks you need to perform to maintain existence. This in itself should also acquire a renewed sense of being part of Nature, although our too-often, cut-off and alienated selves in the workaday world lose that sense. We need to regain it, by allowing moments for your Deeper Self to come back to you.

This Deeper Self is now invited fully into sex, to partner with you, as sex becomes a ritual of prayer.

Therefore you may have moments in sex when the strangest thing is actually happening: you and your own sexual partner are no longer alone. Other personages are there. They are your own Deeper Self and his; and also those "selves" that have become a part of you—for instance, men who have departed; gay men who came before you; and your own self at an earlier age. Your boy-self. Your younger self. And even your wonderful, wiser older self, the one waiting to meet you.

Some men in these "sex as worship" experiences have intensely felt God with them, have felt the physical persona of Jesus with them, or a particular saint, or the action of their own father, in a revitalized, gorgeously sexualized form. This is a complete slap in the face to our "normal" competitive, work-a-day world where everyone is at some point put down to be interchangeable and dispensable. Here you have reached the final "bottom line" of your own value, and it's beautiful. You are unique here; you *are* yourself. Here we are bringing the sacred, the unique, the personal, directly to us, in a form that is as real as our own sexual feelings, energized by the powerful, full, Universe-embracing flow of desire.

20 Words to Think About: Prayers of Sex

"The erotic functions for me in several ways, and
the first is in the power which comes from sharing
deeply any pursuit with another person."

Audre Lorde

Some of you may find that there are other things that need to be said
during sex, besides the "Oh, yeah, do that again!" and the often loaded
expression "I love you." We put so many claims (and chains!) on love
that people are now terrified of it. Love in fact has become merely
another chain: an invitation to a level of commitment that scares the
living daylights out of many of us. Love is now monogamy (for some
of us, that implies *monotony*) and promises that easily terrify, that are
only tangential to our real feelings which should not be limited to promises. But love, in whichever form you choose, is organic to normal and
healthy sexuality. It is part of that sense of both losing and finding yourself, physically and emotionally, in another person.

Since we very much desire the same feeling of love in spirituality
(in a more open and generalized state), having access to "prayers" of
sex is important. Remember that our basic activity in prayer opens itself
up to efforts of pleading, offering, changing, and becoming—feelings
and experiences which in themselves are very sexual. Here are some
prayers of sex that you can either use outright, or adapt as a springboard
for your own words.

"In desiring you, I desire all of life."
"I am the Father that you seek. You are the Son I love."
"I am the Son that you seek. You are the Father I love.
"You are the brother I have longed for."
"I waited so long for you, and you're now here."
"I want to open my chest, heart, and body to you, and
    let you rest there."
"You are part of the God that I want."
"I will allow myself to be the God that you want."

"I have found God in you, and want to be with God."
"I will hold and protect you, as much as I humanly can."
"I will allow you to hold and protect me, as much as I can."
"I will submit my will to you, in trust."
"I will accept your will, in trust."

The important thing about prayers of sex, even when they are not spoken but are allowed to be felt (and this is important, that you open yourself up to the *feelings* that the prayers convey) is that they really liberate a depth within you—and *us*—that most people long to have opened. They either fear the consequences of opening this depth (the fear of shamefulness; of allowing intensely vulnerable feelings to escape, of being hurt if these feelings are not taken as honest and serious), or they can barely approach the area around these feelings. Shakespeare understood this beautifully in *The Tempest*, his last play, when shy Miranda who has spent her life alone on an island offers her entire being to handsome Ferdinand, a man she barely knows, with these words: "I am your wife, if you will marry me;/ If not, I'll die your maid: to be your fellow/ You may deny me; but I will be your servant/ Whether you will or no."

Prospero, her father, recognizes how vulnerable his extremely protected daughter is, and warns Ferdinand that if he does "break her virgin knot" before the ceremony of marriage has been performed, then heaven itself will destroy their marriage contract, and . . . "hate/ sour-eyed disdain and discord shall bestrew/ The union of your bed."

So again we have the experience of desire opening feelings; with the subsequent question: how can these feelings also be protected?

Basically with an understanding that these feelings of opening vulnerabilities, of sexually mingling with and identifying with *all* of our higher powers, are real but this opening needs to take place in its own protected environment. So talk to your partner first about them, and make sure he understands them. Make sure he knows how much of yourself is involved with these feelings. Here's an example to use as a springboard for what you might say. Feel free to use your own words.

"These feelings are not simply about sex, but they go down much deeper in me."—continue speaking about what they mean to you, and what you hope they will mean to him. You can finish by saying:

"So I hope that you will take them as seriously as I do."

Be Creative

Can you think of a "Prayer of Sex" of your own? Whatever it is, it doesn't have to sound solemn and "religious." In fact, it can have a pretty hot, raunchy, and wild side to it. The important thing is that it contains your own deeper feelings that you want to release and share with someone who means a great deal to you.

Write down what this prayer might be for you.

_____

_____

_____

_____

_____

_____

21 An Extremely Important Note About Self-Love

"I proceed for all who are or have been young men,
to tell the secrets of my nights and days . . . ."
Walt Whitman, "In Paths Untrodden"

In this book I have mentioned—and will further mention—masturbation. I think here it's important to talk about self-love and masturbation. Too often masturbation is used as a way of release, of "getting off" and out of yourself, and I concur with this. Masturbation is marvelous, fun, and important for that reason. It's also incredibly natural, which is why it has been such a taboo for so long in so many societies, and yet at the same time an important part of male bonding (and I will speak about that later as well). But it's important now to speak about masturbation and masturbatory techniques as part of self-love and the road to it.

First, it's important to give masturbation its place in sexuality, and honor that place. There are numerous times in life when men do not have access to a partner or that access is severely limited or even cut off by circumstances of age, illness, disability (including erectile dysfunction and prostate problems), and emotional and psychological issues such as depression or religious repression. In my book *How to Survive Your <u>Own</u> Gay Life*, I mentioned that in a committed, even monogamous relationship, men should be allowed private time, if they want to, to masturbate. This should not be a problem within the relationship. For some men though their partner's masturbatory sessions are seen as "solo cruising," a kind of mental promiscuity they either make fun of or find threatening.

This is sad, because what these men don't understand is that masturbation when viewed fully can also be a road to a genuine self-love that is important in any relationship. And for some men, especially older ones past fifty or sixty, this self-love becomes extremely fulfilling and can make a huge difference in their lives. It reconnects them to moments in their sexual past that are meaningful, enriching, and beautiful;

to a more fulfilling sexual present they may not have with a partner; and to their Deeper Self.

This kind of self-love also opens you up to your entire body; it's not simply about handling your dick anymore, but about experiencing your chest, nipples, legs, thighs, groin, anal area, and even feet and hands in your own way. For many men this is difficult to do with a partner, although self-love can be enough of a teacher that they can go from this to saying to him, "I'd really like it if you played more with my tits, or my balls." Or, "What would give me a lot of pleasure now would be if you'd finger my ass while you played with my cock, or played with my feet."

Many men ritualize self-love and that is great. They make it a time completely for themselves with their favorite "toy," or sex items (cock rings, dildos, lube, etc), as well as certain things they like to wear, like sexy jock straps, work boots, jeans, or a T-shirt that has been ripped or shredded enough to make them feel very sexy in it. This is the ritualized time to go deeper and deeper into the important secret rooms of themselves that they might not be able to enter with a partner; or until at some point they may find a partner.

I will be talking more about these "secret rooms" in the next chapter, but at this point I wanted to bring masturbation out as a way to approaching genuine self-love (not narcissism) as a way of inviting the participation of your Deeper Self, and also as a way toward expanding the love of other men.

Very Important Work

Can you talk about your own "secret rooms," and if you have entered them through self-love? Has reading this helped you think about expanding your masturbation practices?

CHAPTER 22

Secret Rooms and Disappointments; and the Desire to Destroy

"One of these days, unless I watch myself, I shall
be departing in some rash fashion, to some foolish
place . . ."

D. H. Lawrence, in a letter to Lady Ottoline Morrell

As I mentioned in the previous chapter, I describe this process of exploring your own hidden narratives, of finding places that most of the time are rarely seen, as going into your own "secret rooms." These are places that you have made off-limits to your own regular, working self (the one that functions day to day), but where at some point you may meet your Deeper Self, the one who is always there with you. These rooms have a definite holiness and beauty, and scariness to them. Some may actually be *too* scary for you—and you should not attempt going in them without some help, in the form of a qualified therapist. They can contain extremely hostile or complex feelings, and the fact that they scare you so much is an indication of the power that they still have over you.

Other rooms may simply be disappointments: you once closed them off, but have lately gone in them and found that they were not what you wanted them to be. You might have always had a hidden yearning to go to bed with an extremely big man who would overpower you. You did, and hated it.

Or, you might have had fantasies about trying wrestling as a pre-run to sex; you did, and decided you didn't want to do it again. Ditto for erotic bondage games, Daddy scenarios, and/or other forms of sexual activities and fetishism.

But sometimes it's a good idea to look at the disappointment and question it. Is it that this secret room just did not offer you what you thought it would contain; or that you just did not go far enough with the right person? The real thing is the depth of feeling in the room, and that you are now allowing yourself to experience this depth which may take more than one attempt to fully realize, or a partner whose unquestionable trust allows you to enter them without anxiety.

However, some of these rooms can trigger negative desires as well, and I will speak about them below.

The Desire to Destroy

One of the more uncomfortable aspects of desire is the desire to destroy. "Destruction," Pablo Picasso said, "is a constant part of creativity. You have to destroy the canvas's purity in order to paint."

Men often find this in their own barely conscious desires to break up relationships that are actually working. And not simply break them up, but even hurt their partners in the process. Suddenly after huge amounts of sexual fireworks, there is a *real* explosion, a genuine detonation: you are now screaming at him, furious, and ready to *kill* him.

This is not simply a variation on a lover's quarrel, although they come out of the same place. What is happening is that desire is now turning in on itself and making a savage U-turn into hostility. The odd thing is that as unnatural as it seems, there is actually a natural basis for this. In other animal pairings, sexuality often quickly turns hostile. Why is this so?

First because the same hormonal "cocktail," basically adrenaline and testosterone, that fuels sexuality creates a natural tension (the famous "fight or flight" response) that easily leads to hostility. Body builders who abuse testosterone find themselves stormed by testosterone rage: at some point they cannot control it, and many end up in open fights or hostilities they cannot explain with people they were once close to, often leading to huge emotional crashes and even suicide attempts. This same syndrome on a less violent level can develop into the "lover's torment": no matter how good he is in the beginning, there are things about him that now drive you *crazy*. You love the fact that he was so contained; now you find him cold and distant. You love the fact that he was all heat and passion, now you find him controlling, jealous, and pushing all your buttons and stress levels. However sometimes it is not any of these more rational things: it is simply the stress of too many, too intense feelings being bestowed on one person—and the fear of being trapped that comes with this.

Your immediate reaction is to want to destroy the relationship rather than give it some healing "air" around it. The "air" may be just some time alone, or with other friends—a real necessity I feel in any intimate relationship—or even a change of locale. In other words, some fresh scenery to make you see things in a different way.

But the worst thing is that the desire to break up, the drama in it, has a backfired sexual component that feels—*strangely*—satisfying. Certainly for a while. It's like a medicating anger takes over, and you are sure that everything will be resolved by it, even healed by it.

It won't. Why?

First, because your initial feelings of overwhelming desire and love won't go away, and you will simply try to land them on another guy; but secondly because breaking off, often coldly (as in: "I don't want to see him again and explain myself to him. There's no use even trying.") leaves you inevitably in a state of even less completion than you had before you met him.

This whole scenario of increased desire and then breaking up—and admit it, many of us, if not most of us, have gone through it—has led to what is called the "gay revolving door" experience. In younger men, who take this cynically as a matter of course, it easily becomes a constant. They joke about it with their friends. They love to read about it in gay romance novels (of which currently there are plenty). They see it as simply another characteristic of queer life, kind of like brunch and Lady Gaga concerts. But few understand that there is also a *desire* locked inside the hostility that led to the break up. It is a desire that is very scary to open up and reach, but when reached can be even more satisfying than the original "hot sex" that drew you to a partner.

This is a desire to be really seen *complete*, even with all of your incompletion. It is the possibility, wanted as it is, of genuine *nakedness* and vulnerability that really scares the crap out of us. It is also playing with the fire of complete submission—and who will not admit how scary that is?

In classic heterosexuality, the difficulties and pain of this condition of complete submission were somewhat mitigated by simple biological and social patterning: Women had children; men worked outside the home. Men had male companions with whom they could go off and do "naughty" things, like drink or gamble. Women had female friends with whom they could gossip and lean on for emotional support. There were still explosions often caused by boredom, possessiveness, and jealousy, but this simple biological (and concurrently sociological) patterning held a lot of frustrations in check.

(Note: This classic heterosexual patterning has been very much broken down by the feminist movement, which opened up whole fields of choices, possibilities, and opportunities for women. Still, many orthodox, or fundamentalist, religious institutions, groups, and cultures are striving extra hard to keep this patterning in it place.)

In homosexual or bisexual relationships this patterning, and the support that came from it, have, for the most part, not been present. In fact, often the very commercialized "gay world." a great deal of which is based on institutionalized self-hatred, strives to keep men apart. You see this in the grating atmosphere of clubs and gay bars; in the "Next!" attitude of revolving door Internet hook-up sites; and in the lacerating, bitchy criticism and "reviews" on gay websites toward other queer men.

Therefore, staying together is harder, even in our age of Gay Marriage. As one youngish single gay man who had been hyper-successful in real estate, said to me, "I wouldn't consider having a partner unless he was perfect."

I told him he had a long time to wait.

There is always that feeling that in our super-competitive world, something better is out there, and this fuels a hostile component in male desire when desire is stopped at a point of fear, which often happens as any relationship starts to take off. Does he love me as much as I want him to? Is he really a jerk after all? Can I depend on him, or will he only hurt me? All of these questions suddenly pop up after you have given so much of yourself to another man. They are like the uninvited guests who crash the party. They are there, and you've *got* to recognize them.

Also, speaking of uninvited guests, satisfying a desire for one man, strangely enough, easily opens your eyes to the desirability for others. Suddenly they're all over the place, and you can't figure out why. You are totally crazy about Jim, and now all you can see are Tom, Dick, and Harry—even if they just appear for a second within your range of vision. There is that curiosity about other beds—and boys—that has been heightened by the amazing sex you've been having with Jim, a guy you're crazy about. It seems almost impossible to explain, and yet here it is, happening.

The question is how do you deal with these destructive desires—ones that have been trailing you, it feels—whenever you get into a relationship? The answer is by squarely looking at your own feelings toward desire, and bringing your partner deeper into them. Letting him into more secret rooms, rather than closing the doors to them. Sometimes this is very difficult; he may be simply too inhibited for this. He has been told basically, "Sex is dirty," and not even in a good way! So, getting into things that you really want to get into, or need to get into, may send him running.

In some ways, this may not be such a terrible thing: you may need some boundaries around your *own* feelings. And he may be offering that solid figure of polarity—magnetic North—that you need. However, if this is not the case and you are feeling stifled by his repressiveness, or possessiveness, then you may be faced with the choice of either leaving him or "cheating" on him, until you feel that you can come back to him.

However, if he is open to it, bringing this "destructive" element into the sex part of the relationship can be wonderful. You can do this through various kinds of role play, or S&M rituals, really exploring your own dominant nature, your submissive one, or both.

In the section on S&M, I'll talk more about that.

Questions for You

Does this desire to destroy have a familiar ring in your own life? Have you experienced it, or been the victim of it with another man?

_____

_____

_____

Is there a "secret room" of your own that you'd like to acknowledge now? Can you talk about it, to yourself?

_____

_____

_____

23

Dealing More with Negative Desires. Becoming the Bigger You

"America I've given you all and now I'm nothing."
Allen Ginsberg, "America"

Question: What is it that prevents us from having the courage to become ourselves?

Answer: Fear of other people's disapproval.

For many men, their own desire is the embodiment of this disapproval—they are so frightened that other people will disapprove of their desires: Desire is "selfish," "immature," "shameful," "perverse," "hurtful," "harmful," "predatory," "neurotic," and a slew of other pejoratives in all kinds of jargons and lingos. Desire, as we now (unfortunately) say, "sucks." What is important is to be cool, detached, and *always* in control—as you shrink further and further away from the *real* person you can be. How would you describe this person?

Start with *larger, more spontaneous, more loving, open, generous,* and *trusting.* Then proceed to considering being capable of controlling yourself enough to have the *larger, more adventurous* life that you do want. In other words, you are not going to be scared off by the things that you're afraid your friends, neighbors, or acquaintances might say, as well as the older, more toxic influences of your family when they made you feel a lot smaller than you wanted to be.

This is not to say that there are no unhealthy desires (and I will deal with them), but even *un*healthy desires are usually there to protect you from your own fear of the more natural ones: namely, that natural desires *are* threatening because they do involve *real* feelings and vulnerabilities.

Therefore, they need to be covered up by cruel or ruinous ones.

Good examples of these are problem desires—such as gambling, and child abuse.

Men who gamble to the point of destroying themselves are addicted to the adrenaline rush of it—and to the fact that during this rush they are removed from their real selves. They are no longer "ordinary Joe," but an amazing, magnetically appealing guy on the edge of glory, fantastic winnings, or that crazy free-fall into ruin that, scary as it is, can also be amazingly thrilling. In other words, you have put your whole being on the table, and now you're betting on *it*.

The only problem is that there is another *being* there watching you, and this is your Deeper Self. He's watching you, and agonizing doing it, even as you are slapping him away. You are enjoying the pain you are inflicting on this crushed Self, this vulnerable person who at the moment scares you with his vulnerability.

And all men are scared of our own vulnerability. Every one of us, especially as we are sure that vulnerability is being witnessed or perceived by others.

So how do we deal with that?

By realizing that within every negative desire is a positive one. That inside the adrenaline rush of gambling is a real person capable of expanding without that rush. Capable of being himself, if he can set aside all the brainwashing that happened to him earlier (which he might have contributed to with his own negativity), and allow his own real Deeper Self to emerge. This may sound fairly glib considering huge problem addictions like gambling (as well shopping and other behavioral addictions), but what I am saying is that there is a real power within your Deeper Self, and after years of denying it, you are scared of it. It is time to no longer be scared, although you may not want to do that alone.

24 Very Unhealthy Desires: Rape and Child Abuse; Sick Sex and Healthy Sex

When I was a kid growing up in the benighted Deep South in the 1950s and early 1960s, when any knowledge of sex itself was taboo, aside from the "accepted wisdom" that the only genuine sexuality was either married (and in the "missionary position") or with "bad girls" in the back seat, all homosexual activities were regarded as "sick."

In fact, *not* to regard them as sick was considered . . . well, extremely "sick." This was part of the shaming boundary that went around queerness itself. Anything even involving a couple of questions, thoughts, or steps within that boundary was off-limits and terrifying; so "normalcy" was definitely staying safely outside it. Most people could hardly question the boundary, much rather step inside it because of the real threat of violence following that step.

We have come a long way from that, but a great deal of sexual response is still regarded as "sick" by the Christian right, and even by well-meaning liberals who feel that "sick" is what everybody else does except them.

However, I do feel that there *is* such a thing as *sick* sex, when it's coercive, humiliating, forced, and hurtful to another human being, either physically or emotionally.

To me rape is always sick. People may have rape fantasies, and if they want to play them out, fine—but as soon as the fantasy of rape leaves the "fantasy" part and becomes the ugly coercive reality of rape, it is horrifying and criminal. I know. I've been raped twice, and you never forget this. The first time I was seventeen years old and living on the streets of Los Angeles. An older, more powerful man picked me up on a street corner at 2 AM, invited me back to his apartment in a distant part of this huge, sprawling city, and about an hour later was fucking me against my will.

He told me as he did it, "I'm gonna fuck you, or beat the shit out of you and then fuck you. The choice is yours."

I was put into the position which many girls, women, and a terrible number of juvenile boys and young men are put into all the time. Often money is involved—rape victims tend to come from the lower end of the economic ladder, and I was pretty much at the bottom rung when this first rape happened. Like a lot of rape victims, I decided that there was nothing to do except endure it. I did, the whole horror of it. I felt degraded and disgusted while it was going on, and worse afterwards. I left this man's car later that morning, as he dropped me off at the fleabag hotel where I was staying. I wanted to place the whole thing in oblivion. Just blackout. But I couldn't. I couldn't go to the cops either. I knew that I'd be on trial, and I wasn't even sure where this guy lived, or if anyone would believe me, a street kid most probably hustling him. I'd already had a run-in with the police, and had spent time in L.A.'s Juvenile Authority: there was no way I was going to return to that.

Instead, I had to suffer years of anger/rage storms rethinking the event—feeling complete helplessness and defilement. But eventually these passed away, until the second time: this time, I was a bit older, in my mid-twenties, and it was again a pick up situation, but with an older, suave, very successful man who lived in a beautiful apartment in New York's gay Chelsea district. I'd had something to drink, we went to bed, and he forced himself on me with a viciousness that literally took my breath away. This was way past Dr. Jekyll and even Mr. Hyde. I was completely too overwhelmed and threatened even to run away. Later I knew I should have, and feel even worse that I did not. I felt at the time that by running away I would have shown, to my immature self, that I was scared and out of control. By submitting to it, I felt that I was staying in control—again, completely wrong. I was also partially drunk, and that in itself sets you up for this kind of sexual violence—a fact that many men need to remind themselves of before they go out.

In *The Manly Art of Seduction*, I talk about male rape in the context of being overwhelmed by two men in a threesome. Rape is one of the ultimate betrayals of trust, and a horrifying act of violence. It is not fueled by desire as much as unleashed aggression, anger, and brutality. As a victim, the fact that you are now at the brunt end of this can rob you of your own desire even to live—rape victims are often suicides, especially in societies where the victim is judged more harshly than the perpetrator or perpetrators. For years this has been very much true for men who are the victims of rape, especially the all too tragically often incidences of men raped in all-male or male-dominated environments like prisons, the military, boarding schools, frat-house hazings, and other such settings.

They are seen as simply not "man" enough to stand up for themselves.

It is important then to see rape as being sick, as being maladaptive and ugly, and something to confront when you are either the victim or know of someone who is. Rationalizing rape through desire is like rationalizing murder through jealousy—a "crime of passion," something that has been done for centuries through history. It does not work; human beings must be capable of better than this.

Child Abuse

Child abuse is a more complicated negative desire. It is based on imposing your own power on an extremely vulnerable person: a young child. There are though within the arena of child abuse other issues. These can include the sexual seductiveness of some kids—who often realize the power of their own seductiveness and use it (what is called the "Lolita complex"), even if they are not mature enough to understand the full consequences of this behavior. Therefore you do have child abusers who seek out seductive children and then try to absolve their own behavior this way—"She (or he) led me on."

There is also the unsettling fact that kids in our culture are becoming sexualized earlier and earlier—the very sad "Jon Benet Ramsey" situation where girls barely old enough to speak are outfitted like caricatures of alluring adults. This has easily created circumstances that blur the lines between normal admiration for children, their freshness, and spontaneity—and abusing them.

And also how various cultures in our multi-cultural world see sex with younger people in very different ways, as opposed to our own (generalized) white middle-class Anglo-Saxon background culture and its values which for most of the last two centuries wanted to believe that kids were not sexually mature before the age of, say, 21, when marriage was encouraged.

In much of India and a lot of South East Asia, for instance, child marriage was perfectly acceptable until the end of the twentieth century.

This does not excuse predatory child abuse, the kind now too often associated with "celibate" Catholic clergymen or even some Orthodox Jews, as well as other people who have used their access to kids as a road to child abuse.

However, what child abuse really covers up, as much as it reveals, is a very normal need of men and women to revert to the state and instincts of children. If allowed, people love returning to that "natural world" of childhood—and some men and women safely fetishize it in "adult baby" games, or sex games in which, as adults, they perceive each other as kids. Our language of sex is sprinkled with kid-talk and kid-actions, with words like "baby," "precious," "snuggums," "doll," "girlfriend," and "boyfriend," even when you're talking about people over seventy.

Negative desires can be dangerous to you, to your health and well-being, and to your place in the community. There is also now a complete hysteria about pedophilia that has ensnared hundreds if not thousands of people in legal traps based on their computer or Internet use, and even on their dreams and fantasies. We have gone from the classical Greek environment where god was a boy, to an era where even looking at someone under twenty-one in fantasy can get you arrested in some communities.

I feel that what this has created is also terrible for children: we have created a world where kids are now *marooned* in the often violent, bullying world of other kids, with no adult allies at all. Growing up when I did in the South in an earlier era, I had dozens of adult friends. As a kid left fatherless after my dad died when I was eleven, these men and women became very important to me.

I fear that these kinds of relationships are now completely absent from the lives of most children, and if they are still present, they're met with huge amounts of suspicion. I feel that it is important for all men, and women, to reclaim a natural, responsive, and responsible community role with kids. But this is going to take a lot of work, and trust, for it to happen.

25 An Extremely Forbidden Hunger in a Very Starved Time

Here I think it is important to talk about something almost all men, gay and straight, have. It's what I call "boy hunger," that is a desire to reach into their own boy selves and bring them back again. They want to retrieve, re-feel and recreate that boundless energy, curiosity, wonder, as well as the sweet, endearing affections of real boyhood, which, by the way, are being destroyed every minute of every day by the cynicisms of this "consumer/data"-glutted age. In other words, boyhood is no longer an option even for *real* boys. But for millennia, men have worked to have moments of "boyness" after they achieved adulthood, and I believe that authentic adulthood should retain some of the emotional richness found in first loves and crushes, first discoveries and realizations, first goals and accomplishments. When these feelings are destroyed, they easily become perverted into violence, destructiveness, emotional blankness, and a terrible starvation of feelings. I see this around me constantly. It has resulted in an isolation and loneliness endemic to our society.

The Greeks satisfied their boy hunger by worshipping boys. Apollo was personified during the Greek Archaic period as a recently pubescent youth, somewhere between twelve and fifteen or sixteen. "Kouroi," (or in the singular "kouros") were statues of beautiful youths often depicting Apollo. Early adulthood was very important to the Greeks since it was the period of male sexual and military prowess, but by having these depictions of Apollo poised at the threshold of adulthood, there was the worship of a pure energy about to happen, ready to evolve, to burst, flowerlike, into the process of adulthood.

Adult men today satisfy their boy hunger by going crazy over cars—a fixation with teenage boys; by sports mania in which they are delivered back to that youthful period of their own sports involvements; by involvement with a military culture, or organizations like scouting; by serial affairs with younger partners; and by play-acting sexual scenarios involving youthful activities. Boy hunger can result in *pedophilia*, but this is not the same instinct that drives men to want to recapture being a boy. Since pedophilia involves using children, and putting them into seriously painful situations, it actually goes *against* the desire and feeling of returning to boyhood itself.

However, I believe that satisfying boy hunger can relieve some pedophiles of the addictive drive toward pedophilia. This situation is especially found in men of power who resort to pedophilia over kids under their influence: if these men could safely return to their boyhood feelings, it might deter them from abusing kids, and also give them a genuine empathy with the boys they have been abusing.

For many gay men, boy hunger is extremely difficult to acknowledge. First, because for many of us, our boyhoods were problematic, involving bullying, hazing, and histories of feeling vulnerable and in pain. Many of us wanted to skip boyhood altogether and grow up as fast as possible. Boyhood to us was a hardball aimed directly at our faces: as seen in parents who rejected us, other kids who bullied us, and sleep-away camping trips where we ended up the butts of painful humiliating jokes and pranks.

But there is also the sheer, naked sweetness of boyhood, of skinny-dipping into so many new experiences and feelings. So recapturing this and realizing our own hunger for it can be very important. It is making friends with a part of ourselves we have tried hard to push away. I did not realize how deep was my own boy hunger until I was past fifty, and could safely put aside so much of the harm from my own boyhood and see, once again, how excited I became by the good parts of it. Cars suddenly excited me. I wanted to play sports, way above my ability to do so. I loved being out in nature. I would get into this feeling of being a boy again, and go crazy with it.

The experience of being gay, bi, or gender fluid is changing so much and I love that. Many of my younger friends now look back on their own boyhoods with huge nostalgia, perhaps reinventing a lot of it, but still at the same time recapturing that "kouros" part of themselves: their most private, naked, beautiful, and innocent part. This is where the loveliest aspects of desire are born, and the hunger to recapture it should be valued as real and true.

Thoughts for You

Can you talk about your own "boy hunger"? Do you have it at all, or does this idea open up a feeling that you have long repressed?

26 Valor and Desire

In my book *The Manly Art of Seduction* (Belhue Press, 2011) I spoke a great deal about valor and its importance in seduction, as a positive act: that is, seduction as a way of getting men outside their too often accustomed (and passive) role of waiting for things to happen. "Valor" basically is giving yourself enough inner value and control to allow you to face life and its challenges squarely—and therefore with bravery.

In sexuality (and seduction) what most men fear more than anything is *rejection*. The fear of rejection in fact becomes more real—and threatening—to them than the possibilities of satisfaction, sexual or emotional. Valor allows them to face these possibilities of rejection openly, with security, *without rejecting themselves*. The way to valor is through a strong connection to your own Deeper Self: that *he* inside you that knows you so well, loves you, and will keep you centered. As you get to know your Deeper Self, your sense of valor expands. The best way to do that is through engaged time spent alone, looking fairly at yourself and your past, and understanding that, through everything there is someone who understands and supports you: your own constant, loving Deeper Self.

There are numerous way to connect with the Deeper Self, and I go through them in depth in *The Manly Art of Seduction*, but the important thing to understand about the Deeper Self is that it is possible to approach *it* (as separate from the daily *you*) and benefit from its nurturing closeness to you.

Here are some capsule ways to approach this important ally of you:

Meditation, especially guided meditations. Meditation is going to the tranquil center of the brain, the part that we may see as being "disengaged" but which actually isn't. It is the awakened, true center of the mind that keeps us balanced, able to withstand stress, and that also pours out love in its most beautiful, full, generalized form. A beautiful guided meditation is to see yourself surrounded by love, as if it were an element that you could walk on, buoyed by its softness and strength.

While doing this, become aware of your breath: that love, a genuine large, even celestial love, is entering you with each breath, slowly moving through your chest and heart, and returning to the larger love outside with each exhalation.

Exercise, alone or with others. Exercise which is essentially getting closer to your body, seeing how the muscles work and move, engaging the balance between our own lightness and weight, is extremely important to mental and emotional as well as physical health and well-being. It is extremely grounding; it moves you out of depression and feeling isolated from your Deeper Self. Exercise should never be punitive, competitive, and stressful. I feel that you can get into shape to become more competitive (and there are moments when competition can be extremely sensuous in its own right), but turning exercise into a grinding competition, either with your own demands or those of others, can quickly turn you off it, and reduce you to feeling alienated from your own body again. So you should have goals in exercise, but the main goal should be for you to continue doing it. Also, pick an exercise that works for you. Some men are not swimmers, runners, nor sportsmen. But they can get into dance, yoga, Pilates, or "full body" mat work and get a lot out of it.

Getting involved with *creativity,* so that you see yourself involved with the act of creation. Even better, try to turn as much of your daily life as you can into a creative act. This does not mean that you have to wash dishes in a creative way, although some meditators will tell you that even doing that can be "meditative," but it does mean feeling aware, open, and alive to the daily world. I will talk more about that in the chapter on "Desire and the Senses." In the meanwhile, realize that true "creativity" means being conscious of the world, seeing its beauty and excitement as a source of inspiration in your life. This beauty is now inviting your Deeper Self to come out and enjoy it.

Allowing yourself to *succeed.* Along with this sense of creativity is allowing yourself to *succeed*—to feel genuine accomplishment. So many men deny themselves this out of engrained feelings of shame and self-abnegation. They have been brainwashed into their own punishing humility and, sadly, a generalized sense of humiliation. They are terrified of accepting their own prowess and a deeply needed sense of accomplishment. They have been told that to express feelings of self-worth is "arrogant," "full of themselves," and "vain."

No one likes someone who is constantly, annoyingly advertising himself to others, even in our 24/7 world of self-promotion. But you need to have your own deeply felt sense of accomplishment—and that your own Deeper Self, as an ally, is behind this for you.

This becomes that angel speaking directly to you when you're on the bridge ready to jump off. He is saying, "You mean something important to people, and to yourself."

Valor, then, as a way of *guarding* you from self-rejection, may seem like an impediment to desire. After all, desire connects us to our wilder, less inhibited selves—our very *secret* selves—and there is something within valor that does act as a screen or defense against harm to us. But valor is also important in bringing our desires closer to us, thereby giving us the personal strength to lower some of our defenses when necessary. The fact that you are now less frightened of rejection means that desire can bloom. And also that you can explore your own deeper, secret narratives, leading to that heightened state of spiritual consummation I spoke about previously.

Questions for Yourself

Has this chapter helped you understand the importance of valor in achieving your desires?

_____

_____

_____

Have you had an experience where valor was missing, and bringing valor into it would have changed the outcome?

_____

_____

_____

27 Romantic Desires, and Opening Up Depression

"People think I can have any boy I want, that I can point and have. And I would love that, but it's not my reality. So I'm on the app 10 times a day looking, because you never know when you might have that magical, transformative encounter."

Joel Simkhai, founder of Grindr, as quoted in *The New York Times*, December 14, 2014

Putting romance, which seems kind of fluffy and light, and desire, a much hotter element, in the same boat is often questionable, and yet romantic desires are a deeply felt and powerful component of most personalities. I spoke about the power of romanticism earlier in the book, but I felt that it was important to revisit the draw that romantic desires have on us, and what we do to fulfill them.

Basically romantic desires satisfy a need for completion and genuine fulfillment that what we call "raw sex," "recreational sex," or sex without emotional attachments does not, although—and this is a very big *although*—at a certain point, what puts even more heat into hot sex is when romantic desire with all its complexity enters into it. Because this means that you have allowed your sexual partner to reach into a place that is extremely vulnerable to you—that secret place where so many of the keys to your own Deeper Self are kept.

For this simple reason, romantic desires have often been fulfilled in a non-sexual way or a way in which sexuality has been extremely *externalized* (that is, left outside) and kept at a discreet distance. In the past, romantic relationships used letter writing, poetry, and art to express and fulfill hidden feelings. Sometimes these feelings became even more intense through the dramas of wars or other large disasters. What romantic desires do is make you aware of your own incompleteness and that someone else can now be the "other half" you seek. Many men spend their entire lives trying to avoid this rendezvous with their own incompleteness, and end up lost in a fiercely competitive world of hyper-masculinity and emotional blankness that becomes wrapped around a profound state of depression.

Opening Up Depression

Opening up this depression becomes synonymous to them with prying open their most vulnerable parts, i.e., that other people will see the yearning tenderness inside them, people who might not be truly understanding or sensitive to it. They are, in short, terrified of being *humiliated* by their feelings. These men often seek and find a substitute for romantic desire in "buddies," associates at work, even nieces and nephews whom they can adopt. Unfortunately, when their buddies, colleagues, and nieces and nephews realize their own specific needs for more fulfilling relationships, these men often feel betrayed and hurt.

They feel as if a lover has suddenly stabbed them.

Again, what brings a sexual relationship into romantic desire is recognizing, on a conscious level, the deeper narratives with which we all come equipped. These deeper narratives also find keys in many religious expressions, as I have said before, so that desire can become a forbidden "lens" aimed at the very depths of our religious feelings and vice versa.

One of the more blatant examples of this is found in the "Song of Songs," Solomon's hymn both to carnal and romantic love and to God, with gorgeous lines like: "I am my beloved's/ and my beloved is mine:/ he feedeth among the lilies." However, in ancient times, this twinning of the carnal and the sacred was not at all uncommon, as seen in *The Kama Sutra of Vatsyayana*, the sacred Hindu book of sexual positions that posits the idea that sexuality and life itself are inseparable. These concepts are also expressed in a number of ancient Egyptian texts that deal with sex, love, and worship.

Using Romantic Desires

A good way to use romantic desires and invite them into a relationship is to make no attempt to censor or block romantic feelings with "common sense," or the usual cynicism that many men use as a defense, rather than genuinely opening up to their feelings.

Therefore, if in the midst of lovemaking, a man says to you, "I've never felt like this before. I'm going to love you for the rest of my life," recognize that the "rest of his life" is right here. This is not a promise waiting to be broken, but a genuine feeling he is entrusting to you. He wants to love someone for the "rest of his life," no matter how long that is, therefore when you hear this, simply smile and feel good about it.

Another beautiful aspect of romantic desire is Nature, and Nature-worship. Men who are close to Nature often find that Nature itself is incredibly sexual—just being in it turns them on in some form or another. It certainly brings them closer to larger, more expansive emotions. Nature does put you closer to God, and God, in its various forms (and I say "it" rather than "He" or "She") is *Sex*: Merging, mingling, exploding into orgasm, re-forming, resting—sex at its most beautiful and opening. Using Nature sexually can also turn into a calming meditative state, of slowing consciousness down but without censoring sexual feelings.

This view of romantic desire is so far away from the stock Western response toward Nature, religion, and sex (in other words, that each one is compartmentalized separately) that it seems revolutionary. Yet it isn't. Eastern religion has been combining all the three responses for millennia, and enjoyed the result until Western missionaries, always eager to clamp down on any natural feelings, turned the freedom of Nature, sex, and a consciousness of God into a state of guilt, fear, and hatred toward others who are different.

It is important then, for your own mental health and sense of wholeness, to again unify and valorize these feelings, to overcome your past sense of guilt and self-consciousness about them. Sexuality and desire are natural, and a natural part of Nature. We see too often, especially now, the violence that happens when they are split apart by religious or political fundamentalism and puritanism in any form. We need to be responsible to others, but also deeply aware of what is inside us.

28 Desire as an Artistic Element

One of the great secrets of art is how much and how deeply desire is embedded in it. In the Renaissance artists used classical myths in order to introduce nude bodies into their work without being censored by the church or prudish princes. In fact, some more sophisticated princes and churchmen started to collect these paintings as a safe "erotica" outlet for themselves. Music is also famously entwined with desire, as heard in Ravel's "Bolero," or Wagner's famous "Love-death" music from *Tristan und Isolde.*" When seen in this light, art, as a deeper experience, opens up our feelings on the level of orgasm or the extreme heights of ecstasy itself. In these instances art is either a guide to these feelings and experiences, or profound evidence they exist universally.

These experiences of intertwining desire and art are often found in so-called "primitive," "untaught," or "outsider" (outside of art schools) art. Examples of this art are often overtly, though casually sexual: in other words, they are not meant to be "pornographic," simply openly and honestly involved with sexuality. My favorite examples of this are the *mbis* poles from the Asmat tribe in Irian Jaya, West Papua New Guinea. The Asmat were once fierce headhunters who engaged in openly-sexual male bonding. The poles were spectacular sculptures, sometimes reaching 25 feet in height, placed outside huts. Some show men enjoying themselves in mutual fellatio, others have males flaunting erect penises. (For a beautiful display of *mbis* poles, go to the Michael C. Rockefeller Wing of the Metropolitan Museum of Art in New York.) No one told these sculptors that these things were forbidden, although later missionaries tried to make the Asmat wear pants and cover up. (The same missionaries and the Indonesian government also forbade them, by 1970, from participating in another part of their culture, head-hunting.)

It is important in looking at art to understand what aspects of desire are being expressed, and how desire itself works through and creates consciousness. Art is one of the chief universal evidences of consciousness, a fact we often forget that when we merely see art as something materially valuable; in other words, without a dollar value attached to it, something is not "art." When you start to see that art = consciousness, you can also start to value things you do yourself that *consciously* present you to the world: Your own tastes, what you acquire, what you make, the stories you tell, whether written or not.

Too often we deny the value and beauty of these things. They are not "professional," or materially valuable. You won't find them on the walls of a museum. But they are important guides to your own states of awareness, and therefore should be placed within your own, extremely important environment of art.

Art and the experience of art is also important to desire in that it allows us to accept beauty as a means of disarmament: of letting our defenses down. Beauty, whether it is that of other people or other things, does that to us. It is important in understanding the relationship of art, beauty, and desire to see that owning something does not make it more valuable, it just gives us more access to it—and that, in itself, is basically temporary. Therefore people who are driven to owning art, so that it becomes almost an addiction, are looking for something else: a connection with the desires under it.

Questions for You

Have you ever feel an erotic or desire-based attraction to a work of art, whether visual, music, or literary? What was the work of art? What did the attraction feel like?

_____

_____

_____

CHAPTER 29 Desire, Disability, and Disasters

Few things illustrate that desire is more than just horniness and is actually a deeper state of human consciousness than the relationship between desire and disability, and also disasters. The stock and acceptable attitude toward desire is that when illness or disability come into the picture, desire, "naturally," should stop. It is "immature," "inappropriate," and even *sinful* to imagine or allow it. And yet illness and disability can be extremely provocative of desire, in that they pry open up a wellspring of other feelings, many of which may have been repressed for decades: feelings of empathy and longing, as well as some of those very powerful (and secret) personal narratives that I spoke about earlier, such as the wounded soldier waiting to be healed, the healer looking for release, the powerful father and the angelic child.

These narratives reach deep inside you, therefore this connection with illness and/or disability easily reveals the way to the narrative.

In the very repressed Victorian period both men and women sexually fetishized illness as a way of expressing feelings of tenderness. An extremely popular vogue sprang up for women who actually looked tubercular, with dead-white skin, extreme thinness, and even a small amount of fever, as well as for men who looked "poetically" thin, pale, and exhausted. (Women in that period were known to take small amounts of arsenic to "deaden" their looks, creating an "unearthly" skin pallor; sometimes the arsenic killed them as well.) The presence of illness and the threat or approach of death meant that no holds were barred to desire—even if this desire was not actually sexually consummated.

Other examples of this is desire coming out full force in times of war, and urgent moments of natural and personal disaster: everything is falling down around you, and suddenly you're aroused! What is causing this—suddenly so many other feelings are opening up—including panic and fear—and all you can think about is sex, attachment, and an overt longing to be sexually and emotionally fulfilled?

The answer is that the urgency of the situation is pushing your own repressed feelings to the surface. When everything else is falling down around you, life itself becomes more real and compelling.

Another side of this are men who have just lost a partner or a spouse suddenly, unexpectedly finding themselves going ape-shit "whole-hog" *horny*. Being driven up the wall with it. They've gone from sheer grief to this sudden sheer frenzy with lust: After so much "appropriate behavior" and self denial, its eager little head (and you know *exactly* what I'm talking about) is undeniably popping right up again. The question is, what opened up the secret door to these feelings: was it just loss, or a flood of other feelings including desire rushing out, that now are close to impossible to stop?

The answer is that, just as in the case of illness, disaster can bring in another *formality* that allows desire to emerge. I have spoken about the desire for formality—for boundaries around behaviors that allow desire either to work within the boundaries or to strongly work around them (as it might, at the same time, be completely repressed without these boundaries). With illness or disaster, new urgent priorities (or "formalities") are set, and things that feel less urgent—such as the old, normal, "business-as-usual" social barriers—seem pointless. As one of my friends suffering from the effect of AIDS told me in the early 1990s, "The one thing this illness has taught me is that there is no room in my life for bullshit."

For many men in the urgency of illness or disaster, repressing desire also becomes part of that "bullshit." They realize it is now time to grab life by the balls, no matter what anyone has to say about it.

For You

Have you ever had "difficult" desires stemming from illness, disabilities, or disasters? Have you thought about them, tried to repress them, or let them be expressed?

_____

_____

_____

30 Desire and Rage; Desire and Death

"To drown, to founder—unconscious—utmost bliss!"
"Liebestod," from *Tristan und Isolde*, Richard Wagner.

Rape, as I have said earlier, is an act of violence perpetrated on a person perceived to be less powerful, and sometimes less human, that is, unworthy of respect. It is possible to completely disconnect rape with desire, and see it only in terms of dehumanizing the victim; certainly male rape, as seen in prisons, student hazing, and military situations, fits into this scenario. In fact, men who are rapists often admit that they did not desire the person they raped, but what really turned them on was the release of anger and the exaggerated sense of power and dominance that rape allowed them.

Extreme states of anger release huge amounts of endorphins found in the classic "fight or flight" reaction that in themselves can be addictive. An interesting aside to this is how addictive rage itself can be, and often we encounter men who are stuck in a pattern of either barely contained rage—they are always either sputtering on the edge of it—or they are intermittently exploding into rage.

We find these rage-filled situations volatile, scary, and also . . . strangely, compellingly attractive: the unstoppable sheer energy of them. It is for this reason that "get even" scenarios (and I include many of today's pop movies in this, although their plots go back to Elizabethan dramas) dealing in revenge fantasies are always popular, especially with men. The female versions of these scenarios are romances with near-rape plot lines where the bad (i.e., uncontrollable, impulsive) guy suddenly turns good and transitions into a caring lover. (This reverts back to the idea of every girl looking for a bad boy who will be "good" only for her.)

As much as society scorns rape, people of both genders often have rape *fantasies*, and what these fantasies tell us is the seductive power of rage and submission, something that the *reality* of rape is not about, since rape is about uncontainable violence itself. Rape and alcohol often go together, and studies have shown that in half of instances of rape, alcohol was a factor for either the rapist or his victim who became powerless because of it. If you do have recurring rape fantasies, even role-play situations can easily get out of control, so it is important to have extraordinary trust in anyone you are playing with. Or, even more important, to seek professional help with these feelings. Rape fantasies can get out of hand, and it is easy to go from rape as a *fantasy* to the horrors of rape as a reality—of forced submission accompanied by violence—to terrifying real feelings of worthlessness and suicide. Therefore separating desire from rape is a good idea.

Death and Desire

There are two aspects of death that are drenched in desire: the desire to escape or transcend death, and the desire to bring back dead friends and loved ones. In this last aspect, death becomes a huge springboard to desire—to overwhelming feelings of longing for those who have "crossed over."

The fact that this longing can be saturated with sexual desire, as well as feelings of spiritual hunger and the need to reach out and have this hunger satisfied, can become problematic to many people. They feel that these feelings are "sinful" or inappropriate. One of the most beautiful examples in cinema of this is in Alfred Hitchcock's *Vertigo*, adapted from a French novel by Pierre Boileau and Thomas Narcejac called *D'entre les morts, "from among the dead."* In *Vertigo*, Scottie Ferguson, a San Francisco detective played by James Stewart, becomes so obsessed with a dead woman, Madeline Elster, played by Kim Novak, that he tries to reshape a living woman who goes by the name of Judy Barton, also played by Novak, to resemble her: to bring his deceased love back to life.

The truth is that both women are fakes, part of a plot concocted by Madeline's husband, Gavin Elster, to cover up the murder of his real wife. What mires up Elster's scheme is that Kim Novak's character does fall in love with Jimmy Stewart's Scotty Ferguson. And what holds the movie together, and has made it one of the most popular movies of all time, is this constant, brooding longing for a love after death.

The desire to bring back love after death is part of our eternal desire to transcend death—and sex itself, as the most life-affirming force, does this. In Egyptian mythology, the life force was often presented as the erect penis of Osiris, the Egyptian god of resurrection whose cult amazingly prefigures Christian worship thousands of years later, with prayers that actually sounded like later-day Christian prayers. Osiris was hailed as the "lover of my soul," who "germinates in my heart," and who, if you are pure of heart, will judge you as being worthy of being restored to life. We mix desire with death in "Gothic" novels like Bram Stoker's *Dracula*, and its thousands of sequels and knock-offs, resulting in today's TV series of hot young vampires and their appealing, often virginal boyfriends and brides.

Still, most of this only skirts the reality that death does have an erotic twist or aspect to it: that in longing sexually for the dead, we transcend death, even if only in fantasy; so by desiring to bring back desired loved ones, we are in fact bringing them closer to our own Deeper Selves: that part of us that can be directly entered into through desire. Many men find mixing these two elements of death and desire extremely potent, and some of their strongest fantasies include "Daddy" role-playing, involving their own long-gone fathers; or seeing in a new partner aspects of others who have gone. Again, this is delving into our own "secret rooms," which need to be opened with extreme trust.

Thoughts for You

Can you think of 3 to 5 people who are now dead whose memory fills you with a desire either to see them, or have a sexual encounter with them?

What would this encounter be like? How satisfying would it be? How intensely, emotionally fulfilling? And how hot?

Think about this, and if you feel enough trust, discuss it with someone you are actually now physically involved with.

**C
H
A
P
T
E
R**

31

Desire and Dreams:
Forced and/or Unreal Sex

> "I jerked awake, and bolted out of bed, crying.
> This had been no dream. No hallucination. But a
> warning."
>
> *Warlock, A Novel of Possession*, Perry Brass

Dreams are a direct and very authentic entry-way into desire. Not only do our dreams reveal our desires, secret and otherwise, but as we censor less of ourselves through an actual "coming out" process—that is, the process of becoming *authentic* ourselves—our dreams expand in their repertory of desire. We are no longer hiding desire and our dreams become even more of a direct indication of them.

I feel that dreams come in two types: "fictional" dreams and "non-fictional" ones. Fictional dreams are those that we can accept as dreams, even if they have an element of truth in them—but all fiction has to have that element in it, to be convincing even as fiction. Nightmares, the famous flying dreams that many people have (an indication of a desire to be "free as the birds"), dreams with strange characters and settings in them, celebrity dreams in which the famous people whose faces are billboards in our lives come to us at night, dreams of talking animals and visitations from people in the past—these are the dreams of fiction. "Non-fiction" dreams are ones that seem so real and plausible that for those first moments after waking it becomes difficult to distinguish them from actual happenings. These dreams also include what Freud called "wish fulfillment" (*wunscherfüllung*) dreams: dreams in which we become satisfied because a long-desired wish has been realized.

Non-fiction dreams can be unsettling, they can also make us extremely happy in that they often contain the material of desire itself: to have your sexual or spiritual wishes materialized in the dream arena. That is, to have the raw material of yourself stated in a way that is very accessible, if you retain it as memory. Non-fiction dreams have made me wonder about the authenticity of many biblical texts and the origins of numerous myths and spiritual traditions: Did they really start as dreams and become confused with realities? Our own life in the twenty-first century has become suffused with these non-fiction "dreams" that have become actually *real*; a good example being "reality" television, which is not real, but basically an edited, very fictionalized, version of either day-to-day happenings or exceptional, very scripted events (such as *The Bachelor* or *The Bachelorette*).

Even TV commercials, an art form brought to universal attention in the last half of the twentieth century, is a completely manipulated "dream" experience passed off as reality. In commercials, your every wish is attainable, if you only buy the product and do as "we" say you should. Another example of the physicalized non-fiction dream is on-line dating: you can now go through endless pictures of suitable people, whose realities may be light years away from what they are putting out there for you.

In movies, commercials, and online dating, all dreams are attainable: we can become rich, powerful, sexually attractive, or capable of sexual power, young, mobile, effortless (*cool*), and free if we follow the complete "script" of the dream and buy what the commercial wants us to, believe in the script of the movie, and accept the online versions of guys who are now "dream boat" material.

One thing that dreams and sexual experiences have in common is that they all take place in the *present*, and, even in recalling, them the present is snapped clearly into focus. As I have said before, in the nineteenth century a code word for masturbation was "reverie," in that it called forth fantasies and dreamy states, opening the practitioner up to questionable feelings and ideas. The French word for dream, *rêve*, and its various connections to "revelations" or "reveal" show that reverie was also seen as a key to realities that we normally suppress.

Masturbation does put you directly into the present "reality," and while you're doing it you are focused entirely on it, another reason it was repressed by Puritans of various stripes: it stopped you from being "serious," from the work that had to be done, and from taking directions. During masturbation you are now focused on yourself and what you are doing *right now*.

Because sex gathers the present around itself (you are entirely focused on it, time seems to disappear while it's happening), interruptions during sex are devastating. This makes problems like erectile dysfunction truly horrible: the dream-time quality of sex (its flow, its amazing talent to make us both forget and *become* ourselves) is being destroyed.

Interruptions during sex, whether ED or other aspects (guilt, fear, or even some form of violence) destroy the dream-desire-sexual continuum that very much reveals us to ourselves, but which can also, painfully, reveal what we are not when sex becomes pretend, or habit, or anything socially enforced. Men who are forcing themselves to be heterosexual (or homosexual, for that matter) when they don't really want to be, who are simply fulfilling a social role, understand this fully.

In these cases, men often rely on dreams, fantasies, porn, or drugs to allow them to function in a situation they don't want to be in, but feel they have to be in. They are splitting themselves between the dream/fantasy state and the real state. Several gay men who were previously heterosexually married have told me that at a certain point in their marriage the only way they could perform sexually with their wives was to "import" gay fantasies into their sex lives. "My wife never knew I was [mentally] with a guy the whole time I was with her."

The opposite of this are rape victims and/or people who are victims of a very personalized violence that is ongoing in which they hate being a part: they split themselves apart in order not to be located in this reality. They are no longer there: they are someplace else. Someplace where they are safely watching this violence from another perspective. The "reverie" of sex has been destroyed for them—and may be destroyed for years to come—and the "dream/fantasy" is now to be *safe*, and not a part of an activity in which they have been forced to participate.

32 Desire and Liberation, Personal and Political

> "The truth of the matter I believe to be this.
> There is, as I stated at first, no absolute right and
> wrong in love, but everything depends upon the
> circumstances; to yield to a bad man in a bad way
> is wrong, but to yield to a worthy man in a right way
> is right. The bad man is the common or vulgar lover,
> who is in love with the body rather than the soul . . .
> the lover of a noble nature remains its lover for life,
> because the thing to which he cleaves is constant."
>
> Plato, *The Symposium*

Desire is often anathema to politics—especially totalitarian, fascist, or repressive—because desire liberates you to yourself; it also has the capacity to unite you with your Deeper Self, and this alone threatens a regime that wants to cut you off from being *you*. That is, from questioning the "accepted wisdom" of the state, and honoring yourself with your own wisdom.

One thing I have noticed from years of working in political situations is how politics constructs its own desires: that is the desires that are "worthwhile" and therefore "politically correct." These squeeze out your own real desires based on your deepest personal narratives, especially the ones that you are forming as you grow and mature. By this I mean that our personal narratives also evolve and often enlarge as we grow, and the impositions of "political correctness," which often appeals to our very immature selves, stunt them. When politics and religion mix, which they often do in extremely repressive regimes or thought systems, the narratives are restricted even more, even though many people may try to embrace a state narrative or a religious narrative to replace their own.

One of our most important narratives is leaving home to find your own life—that is, leaving the home of your parents to find your own self. This theme is constantly repeated in religious narratives, where prophets and saints have to leave their homelands to be recognized; but in state narratives kids are often asked to repudiate their parents in order to become valid citizens of a fascist or repressive state. The state will then give them a homeland, not their parents.

In either way, desire as a natural element of consciousness, that seeks to question the perceived "reality," is squeezed and repressed to fit an agenda. For some people this in itself is "liberating": they can now safely repudiate desires that once threatened them. They find in being politically or religiously correct a union with a mass of people that they have sorely missed. The pay-off is immediate. It rationalizes all of their problems. As I spoke about in the chapter on "Desire and Spirituality," it has permitted the unspeakable parts of themselves to function in a "speakable," or acceptable religious or political setting.

Even though they have invited God (or a particular *Fuhrer*) in, and themselves out, they feel that the pay off has been worth it. They have been personally removed from themselves in the name of "liberation." "Liberation" can also be another word for what is economically comfortable, and what allows you to live in a place without questioning it so much that you become destroyed by it. Therefore desire and liberation are often thought of in a "bargaining" format: how much of your real desires will you have to throw out in order to feel . . . *liberated*?

The answer should be none of them, but too often it is most of them.

Some Ideas for You to Think About

What compromises and bargains with your own desires have you seen in your life? At what point did you recognize this happening?

CHAPTER 33

Other Important Arenas of Desire: Desire and the Senses, Desire and Emotional Response, and Nature

One of the stranger aspects of our feelings about desire is how much of ourselves we divorce from it. We can understand that desire involves our senses, but then we cut off so much of them. We can understand that desire entails a certain physical/emotional response, often even against our will, in that the autonomic nervous system is also involved (you sweat; your heart beats faster—in fact may pound; your ears can burn; you salivate—your mouth "waters"; you breathe harder and become aroused "down there," and even in other places, like your chest, nipples, pelvis, or navel area)—but do we understand how our own responses can trigger states of desire?

I'd like to talk about that.

And then I'd like talk about Nature itself: how you respond to it, and how it, too, can drive desire.

First though, let's look at the senses themselves, and how desire encodes them. One of my first heart-pounding sexual experiences involved meeting a guy when I was still in my mid-teens late at night at a YMCA swimming pool. What I was doing there late at night was another story, but in those more innocent days, it was easy for a group of boys I knew to sneak into the Y in downtown Savannah, Georgia, and go skinny-dipping in its basement pool on hot nights. Suddenly this man looked at me and I completely froze. He was older, in his late twenties, and without knowing anything I knew that something was going on. Suddenly the smell of the pool, its intense chlorine, completely filled my nostrils and enveloped me. I'll never forget it. To this day, the smell of chlorine excites me sexually. There are other smells that do the same thing for me. The smells of summer: distant smells of gasoline and hot road tar, backyard wienie roasts, old-fashioned Coppertone suntan lotion, Mennen deodorant. The smells of fall—burning leaves, quilts fresh from cedar chests, wool sweaters, the sweat from raking leaves outside. Of winter: wood-burning fireplaces, the scent of warm showers and cold rooms, of warm bodies under blankets. And spring—doesn't everything wonderful smell of spring?

Smells reach into us, and bring us back to places, times, and people. Some of our deepest memories are olfactory ones, the memories of the way individual men or women smelled, or of foods and the kitchens and houses they came from. These reach very deeply into our Deeper Selves, without us even trying consciously to control the feelings attached to them.

There are also "bad" smells that for some people are extremely erotic: real crotch odors and foot smells, armpits and other hairy places, and backsides. Napoleon supposedly (it may be apocryphal) wrote his famous line to Josephine after the battle of Marengo: "Home in three days. Don't wash." The French are famous for finding "distasteful" smells enticing, and now in our era of completely canned smells (everything must be deodorized), or corporatized substitutes for actual smells (my favorite is "new car" smell—your can buy it; or "elevator smell," you can buy that too), realizing that you like a taboo smell can be . . . well, fabulous.

Just don't share it with everyone.

Other senses are sight, hearing, touching, and tasting. Desire can be attached to any of these, but the important thing is which part of your own consciousness, your own Deeper Self, will be opened up by them? One of the strongest sense triggers is the sound of a lover's voice, or a man's voice that you find so provocative, so enticing that it doesn't make a difference what he looks like. The flip side of that is a good-looking man with a voice that annoys you or turns you off completely. Sometimes it's not even the sound of his voice as much as that he repeats the same thing until it starts to sound like a whine.

What do you do with guys like this? An interesting solution is to try using a mouth gag on him during sex—to give him the idea that you are more turned on by him not talking than talking. Another thing is to reward him when he doesn't repeat something that bothers you: "I'm glad we got off that subject [or "loop"]. Why don't we try something really different that you'll like?"

You can be more direct and say: "I can't pay attention to what you say while I'm sucking your cock."

Lines like that have been known to get results—especially if you were previously too inhibited to say it. The important thing is that as you become more sensitive to your senses, meaning that you are steadily opening up a lot of yourself, you are also encouraging desires that you censored before. The desire to let your whole body, and mind, feel sexual and sensual. The desire to relax your guard and experience life wholly.

One way to do this is also through guided meditations. Close your eyes and imagine yourself walking naked through an open field that gives way to a seashore. Imagine being barefoot and the lush ground beneath you. Imagine the feeling of field flowers softly brushing your legs, thighs, and genitals. Of walking through a deep meadow with tall grasses up to your chest. Smelling the wild scents of the fields, of the salt beach approaching. Or of a lake, and the scent of lake water, of swimming among lily pads.

Using practices like this opens you up to the world of the senses and the deeper realm of the imagination below it; and of course to the amazing welcoming and nourishing Deeper Self, waiting to experience these pleasure with you there.

Ideas for You to Explore

Do you have a favorite sense or sense trigger that you'd like to talk about? Jot down a few words about it.

_____

_____

_____

Do you suppress any of your senses? Why do you think you do it?

_____

_____

_____

Are there sensual things you'd like to experience more?

_____

_____

_____

Part Two
Practicum:
Expressing
Desire
Successfully

34 It's Time to Get Bigger than You Think You Are (Or How to Save Your Own Life!)

It is no secret now that a great deal of life has been working to contract us, to make us smaller through fear. Part of that comes from the large economic environment we live in—one of constant economic insecurity—as well as our fears of terrorism, crime, and "weirdness" (that is any aspect that makes us feel "uncomfortable" or nervous), accentuated by the media to an almost cartoonish point. There is also the fact that the Internet and the smartphone culture we live in easily cuts us off from a genuine physical or even social connection with others. So it is easy to see strangers as suspect or enemies. You cannot "read" them anymore because buried in their own "digital media world," they don't offer you enough to read.

This has led us to a strange environment where a generalized "dumbness" is encouraged because it seems both easy to navigate and safe. Adults all the way up to their 50s and beyond enjoy acting like kids now; "acting adult" carries little reward to it, especially since the term "adult" carries a lot of baggage with it, as in "adult movies," "adult content," etc. Having the social handles to connect with people has become more and more difficult, and the lack of these handles is too intimidating to approach.

This has delivered us *smack-dab* into our current infantile celebrity culture—in that "celebs," of course, can meet anyone because they are *famous*. They are like the popular kids in kindergarten whom everybody knows because they *are* popular. They also have an endlessly satisfying social and/or sexual life that is promoted constantly in supermarket magazines that create the A-list, the B-list, and the C-list, while you feel easily enough that you'll always be on the Never-Gonna-Be! List—closing off for most people all roads to adventure and a genuine connection to life.

In the middle of all this, whether we want to admit it or not, we still have desire.

For centuries, desire opened up forbidden roads to others, whether the desire was recognized or not. Men went into jungles not simply because they wanted gold, but often because the natives represented a natural wildness that secretly enchanted them. One way to repress their own attraction to this wildness was through the restrictions of Christianity, and, as was seen in novels and movies for ages, those prim missionaries had to do their *darnedest* to straight-jacket the natives, suffocate them in heavy Western clothing, then shove dogma down their throats, all just to keep the locals at arm's length from them.

Now we have the question: how do you get back to that wild hard-on of submerged desire that you've buried for so long (even at the price of burying yourself), while at the same time enlarging yourself enough not to be afraid of it?

I will answer this in the next several chapters.

35 Learning to Be Grateful for Yourself

"Unbiased, oral, and open debate of man-manly
love has been until now kept under lock and key. . . .
Hatred alone has enjoyed freedom of speech."
Karl Heinrich Urichs, 1868,
in "Gladius Furens" ("Raging Sword"),
the first pamphlet published under his own name
after a lifetime of campaigning for freedom for
"Urnings," his term for men loving men

Oscar Wilde surely would have said it: "A little humility goes a long way."

In fact, often hiding behind that prim, self-satisfied humility (and modesty!) is a flaming narcissism that's scarier than any kind of pride. For centuries, hyper-religious and rigidly patriotic people have hidden behind that humility while perpetrating horrific crimes. This is not to say that there are no people of real godliness and scruples, but in the lives of genuine saints you find an aggressiveness that puts many generals to shame. In other words, if you are going to do good, you had better make no bones about it. It is something that you set about to do, because in fact, it's what you really *are* all about.

This attitude goes in spades for politics, the arts, the sciences, and in any other pursuit where originality has to beat out the nay-sayers who will keep repeating until you're dead, "Who the hell do you think you are?"

In the manly pursuit of desire and love, you need to take the same attitude—so the only prisoners you are taking are your own fears, your self-abnegation, and your cringing before the lies of others.

So right now, before anything else, I'm going to ask you to be grateful for yourself.

To be grateful for everything that has happened to you, and that you have survived. And not only survived, but even overcame obstacles (and all the odds against you), and are better for it. And also, be very grateful that you have meant something important to some people, even if it's only to one person: *yourself.*

So don't be ashamed of puffing yourself up a bit, and, like I have asked you to be, grateful for being the big person you *are* capable of being.

Once you recognize this Big Person who resides inside you, you can let him out to find and, also, embrace a larger world. But there are many things that have been holding you back.

Here is a list of only some of them:

Your fear of appearing awkward, "uncool," and out of control.
Your fear of other people seeing you in a bad light.
Your fear of embarrassment—any form of it.
Your fear of rejection: by anyone.
Your fear of really asking for acceptance and/or love; and/or offering your own real desirability.
Your fear that other people will not see how beautiful you are, because at this stage you can't see it.
Your fear of approaching strangers.
Your fear of spending money and being broke.
Your fear of failure.
Your fear of being vulnerable, and open to hurt.
Your fear of not being allowed "in."
Your fear of being thrown "out."
And finally:
Your fear of other people penetrating your "secret space," that is, the places where not only do your own insecurities stay alive, but also the places where you keep your deepest desires: those "dirty" secrets that at some point you may discover other people have as well, and are just as frightened of letting out as you are.

I am going to smash all of these fears once and for all by giving you the key to your own life. (I know, because it's been the key to mine.)

I am going to give you the formula that will change all of this.

THE FACT THAT YOU ARE ALIVE AND ARE CAPABLE OF MORE GROWTH (even more than you are aware of right now) MEANS THAT MISTAKES (no matter how big they may seem) CAN BE OVERCOME, AND YOU CAN STOP BEING AFRAID.

Growth means being able to see, understand, and react. Fully. On your own terms. Without other people telling you how to do it. Everything that enables you to do this, adds to your growth. Everything that does not, detracts from it.

What detracts from your growth:

If you've been the victim of conservative fundamentalist religious beliefs telling you how to think, feel, and see others, it has detracted BIG TIME.

If your parents felt that you were more a part of their agenda than a part of yourself, they have fucked you up plenty.

If you have "good" friends who manipulate you through guilt, you know what I'm getting at.

If you pick your boyfriends, partners, or even one-night-stands (a.k.a., "tricks") because they ask nothing from you and offer the same thing night and day, then it's bad news.

If you pick your boyfriends, partners, and/or those same one-night-stands ("tricks") because their "neediness" insures that they'll keep you around, you're stalled on the same track.

Or, if you pick them because they are abusive to you and their abuse reminds you of your parents (our first, and biggest model for relationships), you are trapped in the same tar pit.

It's time not only to let go of all this, but to realize that you are as capable of growth as this book wants you to be.

So it's time to become as big as you really are, by looking at what is around you and letting go of what does not allow you to be that bigger person.

It's time to come to terms with this simple question:

WHY NOT SIMPLY TELL THE TRUTH?

(In other words, what's holding you back from it—certainly from telling the truth to yourself?)

Or, as I learned as a child growing up in the completely segregated South of the 1950s and early 1960s, a place where endless social formalities covered up the most horrible crimes and evils perpetrated against innocent people: We are taught to use the most complicated lies in order to cover up the simplest truths.

The simplest truth is that your desires are an amazing, miraculous, organic part of you, and also that your own desirability will increase as you get closer to them. That is, don't reject them, and learn how to respect and love yourself in the process. The main route to genuine love and respect comes through your own Deeper Self, and hopefully you have already started to connect with that.

36 Desire and Friendship

One of the strangest and often most difficult—or *uncomfortable*—intersections in life is the crossroads where friendship and desire meet.

("Uncomfortable" is a term I don't like. I'm not sure we're supposed to be all that damn "comfortable" through most of our lives. Sometimes I feel we're supposed to be above our own *comfort*, and actually be moved or *changed*).

In my own youth, back in the 1960s and 1970s, this meeting of friendship and desire was not as feared and disowned as it is today. Part of that was simply the fact that sex had not been as highly tainted with fears of disease, abuse, harassment, and humiliation. There was the problem of being attracted to a straight man and sometimes working on that attraction (something I described in *The Manly Art of Seduction*) and at some point finding it blow up in your face (or not), but the idea of mixing romance (that is the desire to have a connection that completes yourself, making you feel better) with friendship did not seem so foreign. Friendship has now moved so far into the realm of "networking" (in other words, what can *you* do for me and, in turn, what *I can* do for you?) that desire has been kicked straight in the ass out of it.

Therefore, mixing any sexual feelings with friendship has become especially threatening, even explosive. It has also placed friendship more and more in an environment of work and professionalism, so that bringing any kind of sexual flavor into it is now strong grounds for "sexual harassment" charges.

What this has done, especially for many gay men, is to turn too many of our friendships into bland, unsatisfactory things resembling entire meals made up of "party foods," such as snacks, chips, dips, and various forms of high-carbo treats known as "doodles." Of course for a lot of people, these do constitute a "real" meal which is why you have a lot of bloated, stuffed, fat, unhappy guys walking around, many of them barely able to confront their own wet-dream fantasies about desires that will never be fulfilled.

What this means is that fulfilling friendships, like fulfilling meals, need some kind of "formal" basis for them to be truly satisfying. Just as there is a difference between standing up rushed and eating and sitting down, calmly, and enjoying it, allowing desire to *formally* enter a friendship can be totally voluptuous—as long as the framework of the friendship is sensitive enough to both parties to keep hurt feelings out.

Therefore, this kind of friendship requires a formality of feelings, that is a genuine recognition of them, not found in the normal array of bland, casual social networking connections (as in your 2,000 Facebook friends, none of whom you'd recognize at a bus stop) or the kind of business arrangements where genuine feelings are definitely stopped at the conference room door. (So much so, that once you leave your place of employment, all "relationships" there end.) This kind of formality of feeling also goes back to one of the main deeper, secret desires we have: for formality itself.

In other words, you do want to make a definite situation out of what *definitely* was not one.

I describe much of friendship now to be abbreviated to one single word: "Use." That it is tragic. American life has basically become a society of lonely people rushing headlong into strictly-business formatted relationships under the guise of romance, and pushing real desire as far away from themselves as possible. It has also resulted in a situation in which for many men the only relationships they have are variations on the "customer relationship." In other words, they have relationships with "professionals": their lawyer, therapist, working colleagues, or, if they are lucky, their neighbors—or, to put it frankly, most of these "relationships" are strictly boundaried by credit cards and checking accounts.

All of this is to establish your constant credentials in the "Regular Guy" club, meaning someone who can be counted on on a legitimate, business level.

But desire, as a road into your Deeper Self, takes you away from "regular guyism," and into an area of your most closely held secrets and feelings. Into that marvelous, but not always "comfortable" place where you encounter both the victories and difficulties of your own history, the delights of being you, and also the joys of what is around you.

Therefore, let us formalize friendship with these declarations. Keep them on hand. The next time you meet or call a potential friend, that is someone you want to invite into the more guarded territory of your Deeper Self, tell him:

"I want to be friends with you."

"I want to get to know you."

"I want to explore things with you."

"I want to see life with you."

And, when the time comes, and you and he feel that you want it:

"I'd like to expand (or explore) the intimacy of this friendship."

What this leads to can be described as a new category of friendship: Sex-friends. Some of you may already characterize this as "friends with benefits," but, the truth is, I want these friendships to go further. To allow both you and your sex-friends to open up some genuine, new beautiful vistas within yourselves.

So sex-friends are not fuck-buddies, but guys you feel comfortable and loving enough to have sex with, and yet who may not be "husband" material, especially in our age of Extremely Serious Gay Marriage. Although some younger men may go into sex-friendships as a preparation for this, in truth you may have a degree of fun and play with a sex-friend that you won't have in a husband situation when the two of you are neck-deep in real estate debt, and trying to negotiate the rest of life's travails—although there really needs to be some sex-friendship in these "serious" relationships as well.

Seeking Age Appropriateness

Also, it's a good thing in sex-friendship to be "age appropriate." That is, your sex-friends should be close to your own generation. This way you have a whole raft of words in common, jokes in common, and fun in common.

If you have always gone after older or younger guys for "serious" play, a new sex-friendship can open you back up to the joys of staying within your own history and also—and this is very important—for developing *erotic play* around your own body. Some younger men are actually blind to the beauty of guys their own age, and the same thing happens with older men: sex-friendship restores that. For older men who are now finding themselves alone, erotically and emotionally, in the process of aging, sex-friendship can be really galvanizing. It means that you are now recognizing the sexual potential of your own mature body and that of other older men.

Younger men have problems with this idea of sex-friendships, because while on one hand they find other young men rocket-hot, the old demeaning "trick" category full of shame and embarrassment slams in too hard and too fast. It asks, "If I go to bed with you, will that demote you to a 'trick,' that is, a passing sexual interest that I can now discard?" So a lot of younger men who are very used to fast-food sex (and we all know what that is, right?) will find the beautiful rituals around sex-friendship too complicated and not worthwhile for them. Why bother unless someone is pure "hubby" material? Also, if their overtures toward sex-friendships fail, and they strike out completely, they will end up staying tied to Grindr and other quick-fuck-me sites, even if they just stay home and tuned in, with one hand furiously busy as the other holds the phone.

Here are some important aspects of the *Sex-Praktis* of sex-friendship (in other words, the actions of what the Greeks would do).

Breaking bread: with a sex-friend, a meal can be a wonderful way to segue into sexual play. It is a beautiful ritual of sharing, and you might want to orchestrate it in the form of a picnic outside, or a late night dinner—something close, casual, and yet really beautiful. For some men the sheer intimacy of actually sharing a meal, rather than splitting a bill at a restaurant, is intimidating. In *The Manly Art of Seduction*, I talked about the sheer seductive power of inviting a man home for a meal and sharing it with him. A sex-friendship can be explored and enriched by sharing food.

Cocooning: getting very close to each other, in an extended cuddle. The sexual extension of this is "sixty-nining" (mutual fellatio), which may not happen for a while, but cocooning itself can be wonderfully satisfying. Especially if it involves kissing, touching, and simply caressing.

Holy foolery: The Russians, before the Revolution, revered men they considered to be "holy fools," that is ones whose natural goodness, sweetness, and pure naiveté placed them closer to God than those ruled by their brains and guile. So establish some moment with a sex-friend when you can be purely crazy together, like going bowling before or after sex, or playing some crazy kids games like "Twister." Naked.

Dating and sex-friendship. There is a fine line between the formality of dating and sex-friendship. That is, a sex-friend can become a "date," although usually in this arena, dates are a lot more *formal*, serious, and even nerve-wracking. Therefore, you might not want to invest all of those nerves and fears into the casual delights of a sex-friendship. However, if the two of you do start to feel that the friendship has "strayed" into a genuine and serious romance, then you might want to think about actually "dating" him, that is, making some effort to really invest in both the time you spend together and the future of the relationship.

However, I can attest that making a sex-friendship into a deep romance can be difficult if it comes out of left field and is unexpected. So tread carefully there.

What sex-friendship also establishes, and I think this is important, is that being sexually attracted to your friends—in fact, picking them because you find them, simply enough, attractive, for whatever reason—is not nearly as bad as a lot of "experts" would have us believe. This doesn't mean that you have to be attracted to all of your friends, but why not have some of them there simply because you do find them *beautiful*. If you become open to the possibility of this, the opposite can also be true: that by opening friendship itself up to desire, many men you once counted as being completely out of the realm of desire may also now be included in it.

Because now your life is no longer pigeonholed into *asexual* friendships, "husband" material, and meaningless acquaintances. This may make it a little "messier," but in the end more satisfying. Also, you will find that as you develop more sex friendships, the road toward a genuine husband may get shorter—and more accessible. After all, as I have said, there is no law that keeps sex friendships from developing into more serious relationships.

This will also minimize "friendship shame," the shame that artificial friendship limitations impose on you, when you really are attracted to a friend, or a potential one, but have no idea how to extend the friendship sexually. For some men, even the possibility—the thought of doing so—makes them ashamed. So, bringing down this level of friendship shame will make a relationship with a friend much more glowing, attractive, and possible.

In truth, not all friendships are meant to be sexualized. But since we live in an age of extreme isolation (what has been dubbed the "bowling alone" phenomenon), opening up a friendship to desire can be a beautiful change.

Ideas for You

What would you like to find in a sex-friend? What qualities would you look for?

_____

_____

_____

Do you have anyone in mind who has these qualities?

_____

_____

_____

37 Making a Plan: Sex-Friends Circles

When I was younger, I was involved in several instances of what I'd now call "sex-friend circles." Of course back then, in the storied 1970s, we didn't call them that; they were simply guys who were your friends with whom you liked having sex. Sometimes the sex was done in couples, threesomes, or foursomes, as in two couples regrouping, but the basic reality of these circles which often consisted of four to eight guys, was that sex was just a natural extension of our affection for each other, and the idea of becoming a committed couple with one of the guys was pretty distant from our minds. In other words, we were all single men who enjoyed being single, with the exception of one or two couples who simply enjoyed the freedom of fooling around with guys they genuinely liked and were physically attracted to.

For many younger men, the idea of doing this seems as menacing and foreign as taking up habitation on Mars (actually that be might *less* menacing and foreign)—now in our era of gay marriage, new STD's, and incredibly tense social situations. The same men who would think nothing of, say, going to a regular sex party or meeting slews of guys on Grindr, would find the idea of actually being part of a circle of sexually involved friends difficult to imagine. However, a now defunct group called The Loving Brotherhood, headquartered in Plainfield, New Jersey, for several decades promoted sex among friends as natural, warm, and supportive. It put out a newsletter, hosted parties and cultural events, and brought in people mostly by word of mouth or through ads in local gay papers. What The Loving Brotherhood strove to do was break down the isolation of many gay or bisexual men living in the New Jersey and Pennsylvania suburbs and in other rural settings; but to do so with deeper, more affectionate and satisfying attachments than what is normally accomplished now through "networking."

Some people might feel that a group like that simply represented a more romantic time, when men and their schedules were less stressed. The group also fostered having sexual friendships not bounded by racial or class lines, an idea prominent in many earlier groups that accepted an underground brotherhood of all queer men. Still the concept of forming a circle of openly sexual friends should appeal to a lot of men today. Straight couples do this, somewhat, with "swinger circles" that include suburban swinger parties, although hetero swinging has more rules than gay sex circles. For instance, swapping phone numbers is frowned on at swingers parties, male homosexuality is usually strictly forbidden but female bisexuality is encouraged, especially if it leads to two-women-and-one-man threesomes; still despite these strictures, swinging is on the rise with straights. But I feel that at this time, when so many gay men feel cut off from any genuine sense of community, bringing back this type of group relationship can be emotionally healthy.

How do you start a circle of sex friends?

First, consider what kind of circle you want—should some couples be allowed, or should it be limited only to couples or singles? Should there be an age category, or should it be open to a large range of ages? Should it be restricted to men who live close-by, or more open to allow others to participate?

Now think of a name for your group. It can be very loose, like "Charlie's Guys," or "Indoor Adventures."

Once you have a name, consider how to advertise or promote it; that is, if you actually want to do that so openly. You might simply want to start at a local bar, and tell some people that you are thinking about forming a men's "affinity" group that would include intimate contacts. "Affinity" is a good word: it means that men are brought together under some kind of common bonding. Previously, in *The Manly Art of Seduction*, I talked about how to approach men in bars and deal with their sense of protective territorialism.

For some men, the idea of a group involvement may be more territorially offensive than dealing with one man. However, many guys may find the idea of a group to be more manageable than dealing one-on-one: the relationship becomes more generalized, less focused on simply one other individual, offering variety yet with more intimacy and closeness than you would find at a bathhouse or an anonymous sex party.

What you are not doing is simply hosting an orgy or a sex party; in fact what you are doing is bringing several men into your life with whom you can feel sexually comfortable and happy. And hopefully, they will feel that way as well.

I would love to have more activism involved with this idea—because it has a lot of political ideas in it as well. As gay men, despite the Internet, become more cut off from each other and less able to form supportive links with one another, a viable chain of sex-friendship circles could be important to our emotional and psychological well-being. There are large numbers of gay men who feel that they have few if not any close friends. They have working friends, networking friends, bar friends (maybe), and hook-ups, but injecting desire into friendship could add an emotional component they are looking for, and need.

Questions for You

Does the idea of a sex-friendship circle appeal to you, or bother you? What are your feelings about it? If they are negative, can you ever see your feelings changing?

_____

_____

_____

38 Candy Is Dandy, But Sex Won't Rot Your Teeth

"What you want to do is make sure he doesn't feel manipulated, pressured, or pushed."
The Manly Art of Seduction, Perry Brass

The discussion about circles of sex-friends also brings up the issue: how do you turn social situations into sexual ones? That is, once you do find your circle of friends, even if it starts with only one friend, how do you comfortably, but still suggestively turn a meeting into a sexual one?

Again, as in *The Manly Art of Seduction* when I talked about coming up with the "right proposition," the idea is to be as forthright and unblushing about what you want as possible, while still caring for the feelings of the other guy (or guys). In this situation it is important to emphasize that you *do* want sex *and* friendship. That you are not looking for a husband, but you are attracted to him (or them) and you would like to talk about this attraction. You would like to let him (or *them*) know how attracted you are, and also let him know the fantasies you have about him—that they might include:

Sex out of doors, on a camping trip.

Some role play.

Some things you've been thinking about for a long time, and now really want to explore.

And, what would he (or they) like to do?

If he says, "Just get the hell out," you know you've barked up the wrong tree, but there are other trees to bark up, and you should stay aware of that. But sometimes, again dealing with male territorialism—and the generalized "culture of rejection" we live in—he may simply be unprepared for you to be so honest. We don't live in a very honest age, and any kind of forthrightness puts some men off. So, if he does say, "This isn't for me, I want to leave," consider giving him a call, an email, or a text in a week or so, just saying, "I've been wondering how you are, and if you've given my ideas any more thought?"

If he says he has, then be prepared to come up with concrete plans to bring your ideas to life.

"Good. Maybe we can talk about it again together. How about [find a date close to the present—you don't want to put this off]? We can get together again and talk about it. I'd like to hear what you have to say."

The point is, you are being sure of yourself, affirmative about it, and not at all coy. For many men this is extremely refreshing. It also means that you are capable of a genuine amount of *maleness* that men are attracted to. You are upholding your own masculinity and his. That in itself is always attractive.

However, if he says he has thought about it, and is still either rejecting the idea or still unconvinced, the next choice is strictly yours. You can ask him if he'd like you to stay in touch, or just tell him that you are glad he is being so honest with you, and you wish him a lot of luck and happiness.

Thoughts for You

What do you think would be the ideal experience for a group of sex-friends?

_____

_____

_____

What would be the setting for it?

_____

_____

_____

39

The *Really* Hidden Room in Your Own House, or Everybody's Sexy in the Right Light

This brings up another situation that I think is important to include here: if you are involved with a circle of sex friends, or you meet someone and nothing is going the way you want it (he's not exactly your physical "type," he's sexually clumsy or boring to you), what do you do?

For a lot of men, their initial impulse is simply to hit the reject button. That's it. He's gone. You're going to be busy until the next millennium. Work is taking up all your time. Or, worse, "I feel we have nothing in common."

The truth is, if some man is REALLY into you, that *is* what you have in common; everything else is basically window dressing. Most guys don't understand this; they keep looking for guys who like the same operas they do, the same baseball teams, and who makes either a similar amount of money or more. And what they end up with, again, is their own loneliness and frustration.

Instead, what you should be looking for is some guy who is so into you, so sexually right there in your orbit (and debt and possession) that *that*, alone, changes the lay out of the situation. Now you can go through the delicious process of telling him what you want, and "training" him to satisfy you—and himself—at the same time. You can see him as a part of your own most secret fantasies, enjoyments, and delights. You may have to do that at first with all the lights off in your house, but at a certain point, as you both go through the "secret rooms" in your own psyche (and also, at the same time, many of his), you will find that he is now taking on a degree of attraction you *absolutely* never expected.

This again, feeds into an issue I talked about in *The Manly Art of Seduction*: how men we reject become real *questions* that often assert themselves later. If a man offers so much of himself, why didn't I explore what he was offering? Was there something there I missed about him? Still water not only runs deep, it can also contain a lot of heat.

Sometimes it may take some work on your part to go past your own knee-jerk reflex to reject—and, as I say, we do live in the Culture of

Rejection, it affects all of us—but often, on retrospect, you'll find that it was worth it.

Questions for You

Does this chapter surprise you, or is it problematic? Have you ever had this experience of rejecting someone and later wondering about him? Would you be interested in trying the ideas in it?

_____

_____

_____

_____

40

CHAPTER

A Rank (and Frank) Overview of S&M: Order, Hierarchy, and Form

For many men S&M became a joke after they went to their first leather bar and saw too many guys posing in outfits that looked like they came directly out of old Marlon Brando movies. It was "Stand Up and Model" time, and they had little idea what was going on. I know—I was in the same situation for years—until I started to deal with my own attractions to submission and dominance, which are two of the most basic of all human (and certainly male) feelings and desires.

Why this is so goes directly into the male psyche's need for order, hierarchy, and form. Although we live in a culture of constant cosmetic rebellion—every sitcom is now based on the rebellious kid who's actually an adult—in truth, the security of order, hierarchy, and form appeals to all men in one manifestation or another.

So no matter how rebellious, or non-conformist you *think* you are (or try hard to be, with all those tattoos and piercings for instance), there is some primal thing inside you that desires the refuge of peace and protection offered by these ancient male elements I have spoken of: order, hierarchy, and form. It is for this reason that no matter how hard you resist it—or try to—there is, for most of us, an attraction to men in uniform, to the working roles of men (from soldiers, firemen, policemen, lumber jacks, plumbers, and priests all the way up to Wall Street traders, lawyers, or doctors, who are in another uniform: 3-piece suits or scrubs), and to fantasy situations where these roles produce their own scenarios leading to sexual friction and intense heat.

Some of this heat comes from the intense, romantic release of breaking through the "discipline" that these roles represent. For years queer culture was based on subverting power since we had no power of our own, certainly no *open* power. Many of our sexual fantasies revolved around getting "butch" men off their macho pedestals and onto their backs with their legs in the air. Still, the attraction of this close to impenetrable butchness is that it offered to gay men (as it still does to women, and often to other straight men) a resistant enough personality off which to bounce their own aggressions, without being smothered in a softer surface of everyday, meaningless *fluff.*

In other words, no matter how "sweet" a guy is, if he doesn't offer you enough hard candy to keep and attract you, things can end up in a stalemate. This produced for years an illogical attraction: why were queer men so attracted to the very images of men who hated us?

That is, butch, *unfeeling* males.

The answer was that these men offered us a solidity and protection that was absent in the flakey, constantly shifting, sexually-ambiguous situations of the "gay world." Strangely enough, the same male images now offer this to women, even in an age where women's salaries, as a whole, presently out-rank men and where career-wise many women have jumped over men.

The sad thing is that, politically, these same elements can easily lead to Fascism (and many books have been written about the short trip from romanticism to Fascism), but sexually there is *something* about these three elements that rips open so many of our barriers that once experienced, that very "something" becomes hard to resist.

This means that within the seductiveness of order, hierarchy, and form, there needs to be boundaries around them, too. And I will discuss that more in talking in the next chapter about S&M.

Thoughts for You

Have you ever thought about indulging in S&M activities? Have you done so in the past? Are you intrigued by them, or repulsed?

_____

_____

_____

_____

41 Handling Sexual Fire, or S&M 101

"He blindfolded me and whipped me in the most teasing, skillful way, then fed me his dick. I started moaning from pure pleasure. He . . . rubbed his cock over my face, putting tiny electrodes on my nipples and balls, then scraping, licking, and tickling the soles of my feet until I peed on myself. "I became Atman and Brahma, the universal breath that belongs to God. I became the thing that the Egyptians called the *first* light, that glimpse of dawn that distills Creation."

The Substance of God, Perry Brass

Sadomasochism which also goes under the name "Bondage and Discipline" has recently come "straight" out of the closet; the big news was that large numbers of conventional, Rotarian, Republican straight couples were either experimenting with it, or at least curious enough about it to make *Fifty Shades of Grey* into a mega-bestseller.

First of all, of course, we have the question what is sadomasochism, and what is in it for you? Since you have been reading this book, and hopefully getting something out of it, you have probably already got the message that deep within many (if not all) of us is either a desire to submit ourselves to a larger or more powerful force (sometimes known as religion) or to become an agent of that source, as in a "top." The clinical definition of sadomasochism is "the giving and/or receiving of pleasure—often sexual—from acts involving the infliction or reception of pain or humiliation."

The term "sadism" comes from the name of Donatien Alphonse François, the Marquis of Sade who lived from 1740, prior to the French Revolution, to 1814, after the rule of Napoleon. De Sade was an aristocratic libertine who reveled in thumbing his nose and the rest of his body at convention; he spent 32 years of his life in an insane asylum, which was often the fate of remarkably unconventional people, and he wrote openly about the erotic pleasures of inflicting pain. The term "masochism," in turn, also comes from the name of an aristocrat, Leopold Ritter von Sacher-Masoch, an Austrian journalist (1836-1895) who wrote voluminously about the joys of being dominated by beautiful women. His only book that is still widely read in English and has been made into a stage play and movie is *Venus in Furs*.

Although feelings and terms like "pain" and "humiliation" are often at the center of S&M (or *SM*) practices, the core of S&M involves assuming *formal* roles that many of us long for and that have become elements of an almost universal erotic imagination. These roles may be classified as "top," "bottom," "boy," "Daddy," "master," "slave," "dominant" or just plain "submissive," but what they allow you to have is a realized sense of refuge within a formal framework of behaviors that permit some very deeply felt feelings to emerge. These feelings are often so repressed that when they do come out, the force of them, especially within an erotic situation, can be absolutely shattering. For some men, this means that going back to "vanilla," or "fluff" sex is ridiculous. Their religion now becomes S&M, and the truth is, with all of its very formal framework of roles, rituals, behaviors, taboos, and (often) covert actions and permissions, there is an awful lot of S&M in religion. This is especially found in the more elaborate rituals and aspects of Catholicism and High Church Episcopalianism. In fact, the old joke used to be that if you wanted to find a really hot S&M partner, the place to look was inside the pews at church.

Leather is very much a part of S&M practices, and for years the term "leather" was synonymous with S&M. Larry Townsend's bestselling primer on sadomasochism, *The Leatherman's Handbook*, states it pretty succinctly. Back in the days when gays were to be found in sneakers, Brooks Brothers slacks, and cashmere sweaters, wearing leather itself was the costume of the sexual outlaw. There were (and still are) leather bars where leather or tight-fitting military (another fetish) outfits are the "uniforms of the day." These told other men what you were into. Leather and either military outfits or motorcycle wear also revealed the formality of roles, and that even taking care of your leather, wearing it with pride and a display of sexual prowess, was part of your own sexual make up.

You may notice that I use the term "formality" here a lot, because this is the opposite of the "let it all hang out," "groovy," loose and flakey aspects of the Sexual Revolution that turned off a lot of guys. This formality provides a lot of heat and friction because there is a lot of resistance going on. Leather bars were famous for standing, posing, and tension, and that, too, was part of the S&M mystique, because you wanted to know what a guy was into before you committed to him. This was not just going to be a blow-job in the dark, but a whole commitment on your part and his, involving the expectations of—and complete fulfillment of—*roles*.

You were either looking for a Top, Master, Daddy, or Dominant, or the opposite: a Slave, Boy, Tool, or Toy. Age is not really the determinant of role: there are 25-year-old Masters, and 65-year-old Slaves. In fact, being the slave of a young hot Master is a constant fantasy that even the poet Allan Ginsberg celebrated in his famous poem, "Please Master," in which he talked about ultimately giving himself in service to a young Nordic blond master.

One of the hallmarks of S&M practices is a complete lack of political correctness that plunges directly, like a mineshaft elevator, down into the darkest, most secret fears, wishes, dreams and desires of many men. Thus you have black men who actually want to be the sex Slaves of white men, even though, during everyday daylight politics, they would feel this is repugnant; Jewish guys who dream about hot uncut blonde Nordics in black SS uniforms; cowboys who are looking for Native Americans to fuck and vice versa; and strong heterosexual men who are looking for Mamas to dominate and whip them and who even want to be humiliated by other men, while never admitting a single homosexual feeling.

One of the great mysteries and attractions at the heart of leather and S&M is that gender and sexual categorization easily dissolve in this sexual arena. Men who were 100% gay suddenly find themselves attracted, first, to hot female-to-male leather transmen who still come with "original plumbing" (i.e., a vagina), then to dominant women who can make them beg for more. On the other hand, a lot of heterosexual men actually come out into bisexuality or a gay identity through S&M. They suddenly realize that they are attracted to other men who share their own secret fantasies, until they work on these attractions, first with a woman in the room, and then without.

Some other important things to remember while contemplating experimenting with S&M:

S&M involves the whole body, not just your genital regions.

There are parts of you that you might easily overlook in your regular everyday life that can have huge erotic significance in S&M. These include your underarms (some S&M practices include bondage and tickling, which can become an extreme turn on); your forearms, knees and the very sensitive area behind your knees; your neck and upper chest, and of course your nipples (nipple play and nipple "torture" are big parts of S&M), your navel (which I think is one of the most erotic areas of the body), and let's don't forget that beautiful space between your navel and your groin. There are also your testicles and the whole area of your buttocks. Using a light caressive stroke with a small leather whip on anyone's balls and butt can bring them to a state of extreme excitement.

S&M is a lot more than simply "fuckin' and suckin'."

It involves a real exchange of power, of deeply felt often hidden feelings and urges, as well as other aspects of your personality that you may have kept under wraps except in the case of actual duress or emergencies. S&M very much harnesses that basic "fight or flight" adrenaline reaction that most people try to suppress, and it uses it directly.

S&M is not torture, punishment, or physical abuse, unless in an ironic sense you *want* it to be that way. If someone perpetrates a *crime* against you, in no matter what circumstances (in a bar, in your home, or another place)—against your will—then it is not S&M.

For many men, coming out into S&M practices and roles represents a genuine second coming out, aside from their simply being gay, bi, or even pansexual. Conversely, as I said earlier, for heterosexual men, it also represents an evolvement from standard male chauvinism into something much deeper. This can mean giving up male power to a female, by becoming a submissive male, and for many conventional (non S&M, non-sexually curious, or "vanilla") people this is much more threatening than mere "queerness" which they can laugh off or discount. Submissive heterosexual men who allow themselves to be dominated by women are often objects of super contempt, seen as beyond being merely sissies, or even being "pussywhipped." Sissies can't help it, and many men who are dismissed as being "pussywhipped" can't either. But submissive straight men are seen as *inviting* this domination, even though a very large number of men found in "everyday life" still harbor deep, secret fantasies about dominant women.

Using Bondage, Limits, and Restraints

Or, how can a lack of freedom be so . . . freeing, and appealing?

Many men find even light bondage and restraints (such as being blindfolded), extremely exciting because as it cuts off some visual stimuli, it opens up the imagination toward others. Now every touch that you cannot turn away from becomes more expressive and powerful. You are willingly giving up a portion of your own freedom—meaning that now someone else has been willfully empowered to be responsible for your own pleasure. You are giving your trust to him, and this, in itself, is extremely erotic. It also plays into confinement fantasies and roles, such as being imprisoned and having a jailor who is committed to you erotically, or being a slave/worker in a deep Pennsylvania mine with an foreman who heals the wounds inflicted by such hard, humiliating work.

Many role fantasies work on the same idea. We love them because they accentuate both the self-contained boundaries of the roles and the forbidden aspect of the sex play that comes out of them. Almost every man who's been in the service has some story, even on a fantasy level, of sex play within the military; therefore military fantasies are huge in S&M circles, as well as cop fantasies, priest and acolyte fantasies, fireman fantasies, and any situation where one person has power over another, a power that can span from very good to very bad. There is also the idea that work itself, and the boundaries around it of "Top"/"Bottom" roles (executive-boss-manager vs. floor-level employee) once transgressed, are extremely erotic—certainly on a fantasy level. Therefore addressing men in S&M practice as "Sir!" can create an aura of power that is extremely exciting, just as being addressed as "Boy" or "Slave" can be.

"Now, let me know who's Boss."

Your ability to accept power segues beautifully into that demand. You can ask that of another guy—that he will see that at present you are now *Boss*. And he can ask that of you. It means that one of you is calling the shots, while the other is really enjoying it, certainly in this circumstance.

You are willing to give up your own power, and to a certain degree your own volition, to accept someone else taking care of you on a purely erotic level. Daddy-Son relationships are openly involved with this. And for many men, of any age, these relationships are extremely powerful and attractive: they push us out of the "normal" world of the bland, regulated relationships and feelings that are part of our everyday environment. Daddy will take care of you and love you specifically, because you are his Boy/Son. What excites us are specific meanings in a relationship and how they, or the fantasy of them, appeal internally to us. Several men who are good at role-playing and/or fetish relationships have told me that their favorite bondings are Daddy/Son, Prisoner/Jailor, and of course Military ones. That these intense connections explore feelings that most men want to expose, but are very much afraid of.

I asked one of them, "How above love, as a fantasy? That is, the fantasy that you are now totally, completely in love with Daddy, or your Jailor, or your Sergeant?"

"That," he told me, "Is the most difficult of all fantasies because it's too easy to confuse it with reality, and when you do that, things can become complicated and obsessional and most men are scared of that."

However, this does not mean that you cannot have S&M within a love relationship, and many love relationships really enjoy the heat and friction of S&M. It can certainly keep fresh what can become a stale sexual situation, although sometimes it can also complicate things when, say, two "S's" bond in love and therefore need to find either submissives ("M's") from the outside, or one submissive they can share.

Bondage and Boundaries

It is very important to understand what your boundaries are in S&M, and to make it plain that you have them. Trust is at the heart of S&M play, and the fact that you trust someone enough to let him inside your boundaries extends the emotional range of sex play hugely. This is extremely important to many men who either normally have a hard time expressing their feelings, or, have become so turned off by too many experiences of casual sexual hook-ups that these experiences finally have no emotional pay-off for them at all. This in itself becomes self perpetuating, especially in the case of Internet hook-ups: these couplings have become more and more lacking in feelings, and the men involved with them colder and less able to extend themselves emotionally.

Well-played S&M situations by their nature can change this dynamic. Which leads us to the subject of pain itself.

Pain has many functions in your mind/body continuum. It can indicate that something is critically wrong, as in the case of a broken bone, muscle, or tendon problem; it can alert you to a coming danger—for instance, if you extend a joint beyond its normal range, you are headed toward disaster.

Or, it can accompany a flood of endorphins that act as analgesics in your brain. Endorphins are the chemicals of pleasure, satisfaction, and a heightening state of self-esteem. Endorphins also flood your brain during orgasm. So learning how to direct and/or accept a certain degree of pain can become extremely powerful, as long you understand the limits of this experience. Men have become permanently injured and even killed during S&M play. You don't want to be one of them, which means that it is important to play with experienced, responsible playmates.

Be extremely careful with any play that cuts down or off blood supply to an area, or even more important, your air supply. This means that straps, ropes, or other equipment used in bondage have to be constantly monitored. It means that if you are a Bottom, you need to have a Top or Master who knows what he's doing, and even has some training in first aid.

Also, as a rule: Never allow anyone to *completely* keep you from speaking or being heard. Mouth gags and loud background noises can keep you from protesting that things have gone further than you want them to. So make sure that background noises are controlled, and if you do use, or have someone else use, a mouth gag, make sure *you* or *he* can take it off fast if necessary.

Also, it's important to have a "safe word," that tells your Top or Master automatically that things have gone too far. It should be more than simply saying "No," because sometimes you may say "No," and mean that you don't like something but you are still playing within boundaries, instead of being insistent that the time to stop is now.

A good safe word is "Arnie," because it's easy to say, and yet emphatic. Other men like words like "Red," as a reference to "red light"; or "Halt," which is easy enough to understand in several languages (such as German or English). Some men also have a code word for "slow down," or "ease off," such as "Yellow," or "Watch."

What's very important with safe words is that they are understood to be consensual: both the Top and Bottom need to understand and accept them. When one is used, it is accepted by the Top to mean that its employment still puts both men within boundaries. If the safe word is ignored, then the Top is out of boundaries, and this can be dangerous for both players. It can put the Bottom's health and life in danger, and it also means that the Top is acting abusively, if not criminally. No Top wants to get a reputation for this, and if you are a Bottom and you do resort to your safe word, and it is ignored, you should let it be known very fast and loud that this will not be tolerated by you.

S&M people of all genders and sexual identifications like to tell their critics that S&M play should be "safe, sane, and consensual." Using safe words, as well as having a real understanding of how bondage works, how S&M toys and tools need to be applied and taken care of, and how Bottoms and Tops interact, keep it that way.

Having this sense of genuinely safe boundaries around S&M can add a huge amount of heat to the situation. It means that the ancient, extremely volatile issues of control and dominance that excite most men, in one way or another, can be expressed sexually.

"Let me know who's boss!" can be extremely exciting in our world of blander "vanilla" relationships which, despite their outward "nice" trappings, still often carry unvoiced aspects of threat to them—either in our working and/or social environments, or, certainly, sexually. Some examples of these are "perfectly nice guys" who continuously use emotional blackmail to get what they want; "victims" who are always putting you in the "abuser" role no matter what you do; extremely competitive men who play "dirty pool" at every point, while denying how competitive they are; and guys who set sexual traps for you that soon destroy what you thought would be a good experience.

Dominance and submission, sado-masochism, and bondage and discipline are definitely going on here—but without any sexual payoff. Genuine S&M takes these experiences and feelings, pushes all of that "fight or flight" adrenalized super-fuel of desire directly into them, and uses them.

Society still has a hard time with this, even though pop culture is filled with S&M imagery: rock stars and super heroes dressed in leather. Kick boxing, wrestling, and other sports where half-naked men get close enough to fuck each other, but publicly can only inflict pain—either real or theatrical—on each other. American football leagues where the players are dressed to exaggerate super-sexuality (shoulder pads, super-tight-butt pants, protruding cup-jockstraps, etc.) while the crowd screams for them to kill each other. The truth is, these are all just excuses to get normal human aggression out, and S&M provides a sexual venue for it. This in itself is hugely exciting to most men, and men who live within the S&M subculture find that their sexuality now embraces an amazing amount of life, and vice versa.

Questions for You

Was this chapter on S&M useful to you? Would you like to get more involved with this formality of power and roles?

_____

_____

_____

Have you ever been involved with men who used "mental" games or emotional blackmail like I spoke of, that you found particularly difficult to deal with and/or abusive?

_____

_____

_____

Has this discussion about S&M helped you understand some of these emotional games, without the more honest sexual benefits of an S&M sexual environment?

_____

_____

_____

Do you have any kind of S&M situation that you'd like to see happen?

_____

_____

_____

42 Sexual Competitiveness and How to Deal with It

This brings up another question: how you do spot and deal with sexual competitiveness?

First, what is "sexual competitiveness"? An answer for this comes from a really remarkable source: Jerry Seinfeld, or at least his writers. In one of the *Seinfeld* episodes, Jerry's sometimes girlfriend and sidekick, Elaine Benes, asked, "Why do gay men change partners so much?"

Jerry answers: "Well, it's like this, Elaine. When you both play with the same equipment, you change balls more often."

Sexual competiveness can take many forms. Some include:

A man who resents any kind of attention you get, sexual or otherwise.

A man who is constantly inviting attention from others, even in your presence; so that at a certain point, you feel that you don't exist.

A man who is constantly envious of you rather than *jealous*; in other words, he wants what you have, no matter what it is, and resents that he doesn't have it. This can mean any kind of attention from other men, basic recognition from others, or your own looks and talents. If he were simply *jealous*, he would prefer that you both didn't have these things. Instead, he wants them *all* for himself.

If he doesn't get them, he can become withdrawn, angry, or abusive. Often men who are involved with sexually competitive partners simply give in to them. They will offer them whatever it is that they want, until finally the situation becomes so onerous (and there is no genuine kind of satisfaction for him), that finally the couple either break up, or barely communicate with one another.

How do you get out of this?

One way is to direct a competitive partner into situations where he is not competing sexually with you, but investing his competitive energy into games, professional situations, or sports where he can compete and—either win or lose—feel some satisfaction. Once he does have this feeling of satisfaction as well as recognition from being part of a team, a cause, or a project, he can come back to you and hopefully not play the same games with you. This also means that you have to become invested with him in his new interest. Never put it down, but build him up with it.

A good thing would be for you to join him in this pursuit; for instance, you can both join a sports team or a take up mountain climbing or running. (But don't do this if you know you are going to beat him at every point; in that case, join your own team.) You can also make sure that you back him up as much as possible with his professional projects, and that you recognize the importance of his work and what it means emotionally to him.

Competitive men often come from a family background where either they had no affection (or recognition) outside of a sports or competitive arena, or their own sexual feelings were completely hidden while the only possible avenue for bonding with other men, like their fathers, were sports. (I spoke about that earlier, talking about homophobic poisoning.) Some heterosexual couples compete sexually too, but the amount of sexual competitiveness within same-sex couples seems to be higher.

This competitiveness can destroy trust, which makes it harder to go sexually into areas where trust is foremost, to have those experiences of spiritual consummation as well as genuine sexual exploration. Sometimes, cutting through a lot of emotional resentment and sexual standoffs, putting some kind of S&M format into sex can be very effective and satisfying. Turning a sexually competitive man into a "Bottom" or even allowing him to be the "Top" (with some restraints, so that he does commit to showing the necessary respect for you), can explode a lot of the emotional repression he has that he's been using competitiveness to avoid confronting.

If none of this works, it may be a time to bring in other help, to go into couples therapy, for instance. The important thing though is to realize that this competitiveness is not about you, it is about *him*. Or, if you recognize that you *are* the competitive partner, to look inside yourself and see what needs to be done, before you destroy every intimate relationship in your life.

43 Lovesickness without Love

"Love . . . is the source of the greatest benefit to us. For I know not any greater blessing to a young man who is beginning life than a virtuous lover, or to a lover than a beloved youth. For the principle which ought to be the guide to men who would nobly live—that principle, I say, neither kinship, nor honor, nor wealth, nor any other motive is able to implant so well as love."

Phaedrus, speaking in *The Symposium*, Plato

Many people today are in a situation that I describe as "lovesickness without love." That is, they desire real love so much that this starvation for love has left them emotionally and physically weakened. It is very hard for them to connect now and break out of their own love-starved condition. Part of this is that as the level of love starvation increases, the demands on a basically fantasy love-object are also ratcheted up.

He must be so good looking, so available, so *into* you, of such an age and on such a level of personal, career, and emotional attainment that the possibilities of finding this paragon become only slimmer and slimmer. In other words, what you're looking for is everything you're sure your parents should have been to you, everything your friends can never really come up to, and sexually and emotionally everything you've ever dreamed of.

This has led many men into a state of depression: it's like the world of their aloneness is really closing in on them, without any attainable way out. When they go to bars, parties, or other gatherings, they basically see no one and can reach out to no one. Most social situations become only blind alleys to them. Even most of their friends start to seem colder, more aloof, and harder to reach because these extremely love-hungry men are now in a state that borders on being emotionally blank: Emotionally, they are in a state of anorexia. They are starving themselves, except that unlike anorexics who mistakenly think they are "fat," these men realize there is this pit inside them that is empty.

How do you get over this? Aside from a lot of therapy (and antidepressants, if the situation is that urgent), by bringing more real fun and "boy" moments into your life. Get past the idea that every relationship has to be "eternal," headed for the altar marriage-material, or, in business lingo, has to go directly into the "black" after so much expenditure of effort. Make a list of all the things you do for fun, and see if you can find others who are interested in joining you. This means that even if you are not a "joiner," join a group, but don't simply go to meetings or group activities and then run to the door afterwards.

Instead, really go after buddies within the group. What you want to do is bring someone into your own loneliness, and then others will come in naturally. At some later point, many other feelings will start to rise to the surface about men: feelings of trust, hope, and love. In *The Manly Art of Seduction*, there is a whole section on why people form and join groups in order to meet other people. It is a natural aspect of human life that our "online" culture is authentically violating—because you need actual *contact* with other humans. This is important to mental, physical, and emotional life, and also the spiritual well-being that most people seek, a condition which actually means that what they are seeking is their own *wholeness*.

This "lovesickness without love" really violates that, since that gnawing emptiness inside you makes it very difficult to treat yourself as a whole person. What's lacking is too evident. So it's important to bring people toward this emptiness, even if they are not going to immediately fill it themselves.

It also gives you an important practice dealing with real human beings rather than the pretend figures that make up so much of either an online life—if you are used to gay cruising sites—or if you have based your social life on your working life. What is important is to develop connections that have some strength and flexibility because all real relationships require that. I have spoken about that in my books *How to Survive Your Own Gay Life* and *The Manly Art of Seduction*, that your actual friends will give you enough credit and value to allow many of the pressures and problems of friendship not to overwhelm the relationship. This is an important thing to have today and what is lacking in so many online basically "flat" relationships where any kind of tension or disagreement is fatal, because you really don't know these people.

You only know an online shadow of them.

So if you do find yourself in this situation of lovesickness without love, pay attention to yourself and what you really want, then make a plan to bring others into this vacuum, because at some point you will find the right person, and your own Deeper Self will know him.

Questions for You

Have you ever experienced this feeling of "lovesickness without love"? How did it feel to you? Are you still in it?

_____

_____

_____

44 The Sacred Grove of Desire

"He was naked to the hips, his velveteen breeches slipping down over his slender loins. And his white slim back was curved over a big bowl of soapy water, in which he ducked his head, shaking his head with a queer, quick, little motion, lifting his slender white arms, and pressing the soapy water from his ears, quick, subtle as a weasel playing with water, and utterly alone. Connie backed away around the corner of the house, and hurried away to the wood."

Lady Chatterley's Lover, D. H. Lawrence

If there is any kind of antidote for "lovesickness without love" I'm sure that it would be found in the Sacred Grove of Desire, that place where our own imagination opens up fully to embrace what we are. But before I talk about this place, there is a famous maxim that I like:

Every guy is looking for the good girl who'll be bad *only* for him, just like every girl is looking for the bad boy who'll be good *only* for her.

In other words, what every person wants in a "balls-out" romantic encounter is someone who'll lead you into that personal, private, "sacred" space where you can lose all of your fears safely and be your own *real* self. That's right: the *self* you don't show Mom and Dad, and certainly not the people at work. In fact, it is the *self* you are forced at work to leave out—and if you don't, well, there's "something *really* wrong with you." In other words, you are really missing that *self*, but more about that later.

So it is basically the "self" that after years of habit and lots of help from others, you have successfully repressed on your own.

This real *self* (as opposed to the Deeper Self, which is actually even deeper than the *self* you lose at work) is also the part of you often repressed to the point of pain that you associate with shame, with past experiences of hurt, with being rejected by your friends, or pointed out in a humiliating way. It is the *self* that you have learned to cover up with your "better" self: that prim, even assertively well-behaved one that represses so much of an authentic you.

In truth, you've been a Goody-Goody for so long that you can't figure out where your own, really "dirty" self is—you remember, the one that's still pretty unfinished and uncool, but would love to have the kind of fun you know is "dirty"?

This is your *real* self with all the "fun" parts showing.

Where is *he*? And, God, how long ago did you lose him?

I describe the place where your own genuine *self* comes out (hopefully—but not always—in the presence of another person) as the *Sacred Grove of Desire.* It is the place where your own *inner nature* merges with both the human race's primal animal nature and its true spiritual nature as well.

This is the place of a genuine, tender sexual physicality, and also compassion. It is these feelings that often unhinge men, making them feel at once defenseless, yet steered to the most heart-stopping actions.

We see these feelings sometimes in moments of extreme duress (a death in the family, for instance) or natural disasters, and in a total surrender to love and spiritual commitment; we find them in that place where we abandon our "normal" selves to something extraordinary. So we want that place to be where we can be completely "naked," on every level (even if it scares the shit out of us at the same time), thus it brings us back to my opening quip about what every boy and girl wants: someone who can strip you naked, yet protect you at the same time.

Many men do not allow themselves to feel that this is possible: They have been trained into their own smallness. We find this especially so now, since our relationships have become so "public" that we instantly infer that every man's lover, partner, or husband must give him everything, even if the everything has been contracted simply to a public statement, as has historically been true with heterosexual marriages and relationships.

So we are now deeply scared of this Sacred Grove. It's a menacing jungle to us, bringing up scores of accusations and finger-pointing. A perfect example are politicians caught "red-handed" in some "compromising" situation, such as frequenting prostitutes, or being engaged in extramarital affairs, or perhaps something as basically innocuous as sending a "sex-text" to a person they barely know but who will join in on the public "blood-letting" of exposing them. They may be hard working public servants, but now they're blasted as "deviants," "exploiters," etc. and no one can even understand why they have jeopardized everything to engage in this kind of "questionable" behavior.

The idea that after being on public display twelve hours a day as the "Best Little Boys in the World" they are expected to be, they may want to wander into their own Sacred Grove, is incomprehensible to the American public. In Europe, public officials are fairly expected to "misbehave." They have it coming to them. It's their own *private* life—something we desperately want to dispense with in the U.S.—but the feeling over there is that after all they have given of themselves to the public, they deserve at least this limited amount of privacy.

It's their life, why even question it?

We definitely don't have that feeling in America.

Another interpretation of the Sacred Grove is that it's where desire, sexuality, and spirituality meet on equal grounds. If what we call "spirituality" is the most private part of yourself—that genuine meeting with your own God-figure—then the Sacred Grove is that place where this level of privacy naturally attracts the other *private* parts of you, desire and sex.

Among Orthodox Jews, mingling desire, the privacy of sexuality, and religious ritual is something met with familiar nods. Once desire is "cleansed," that is made completely "Jewish," it is welcomed as part of the human component that can join God. Thus one of the first rituals in the Bible is circumcision whereby Abraham pledged himself to God—and, by the way, performed it on himself. Orthodox Jewish women cleanse themselves in a *mikvah*, or ritual bath, once a month after menstruation, and certainly before their first marriage night. According to Kabalah, Jewish esoteric mysticism, desire itself contains the light of God, and brings us back to that perfect innocent state of the Garden of Eden.

The idea that the Sacred Grove was a garden, like Eden, or at least a temperate and consoling woodland, is common in English literature. To the English, the woods and a garden are both places where the soul is invited to be itself, gracious, loving, free. Robin Hood's men, whom modern research has found might very well have been homosexually inclined, found a convenient refuge in the woods. And Shakespeare's comedies often take place in or near forests, such as the Forest of Arden in "As You Like It," or the unnamed "forest near Athens," in "A Midsummer Night's Dream." Macbeth is warned that he will not be undone until "Great Birnam wood," a forest, actually moves. Since forests were considered places with souls of their own, the idea that a wood might move seemed impossible. In gay author E.M. Forster's great long-suppressed novel *Maurice*, from 1913, he places the Sacred Grove within the "greenwood of England," that primeval forest where men could go off on their own and be themselves, away from an extremely repressive Edwardian society.

In Forster's world, the greenwood groves were always there, but they became something completely different when shared by another kindred spirit. Although *Maurice* was often seen by readers as a fantasy of two men rejecting society to go off and live on their own in the wildwood, in truth the model for *Maurice* was the relationship of Edward Carpenter, an openly gay Edwardian poet and spiritualist, and his working class partner George Merrill, who lived off the land in the wilds of Sheffield, away for the most part from society. In order for them to live together as freely as they did, away from the constantly prying eyes around them, Merrill was often taken to be Carpenter's servant—although sexually it was the other way around.

Carpenter felt submissive to Merrill, because Merrill had so much to teach Carpenter about real life: the life of feelings, of nature, of the Greenwood that protected them.

It is very sad to me that this idea of Forster's Greenwood, that is, the Sacred Grove of Desire, is dying out so fast today. It has been replaced by the total homogenization of queer culture and sex, and the growing state corporatization around us. The idea that men could go off together to seek the real privacy of their feelings and sexuality is anathema to contemporary life. As much as I believe in the importance of gay marriage or certainly queer vows of coupled intimacy and ultimately nurturing feelings, what has been lost in the Sacred Grove of Desire is terrible to me: that life-changing coming together of men in couples and groups. It is an exchange of energies and intensely held feelings that has not found a real replacement in the queer "networking" of today, when gay men basically try to figure out ways to use each other rather than to share each other's more deeply held personal substance.

This has put queer men into the same state that millions of straight men are: isolated and depressed. Walt Whitman sang openly about male "adhesion," that is, our ability to stick to each other, to comfort and nourish each other. He meant this in what would now be considered a gay, "queer," bi, or same-sexualized context. Now the only context in which most men have closeness is competition: sports, sports bars, and the almost ridiculous idolization of sports figures, even as a few of these figures cautiously come out of the closet.

Sports now tries to satisfy a hunger that is so much deeper than it is capable of satisfying—a hunger for genuine aesthetic, emotional, and even sexual satisfaction. It's easy to understand how the need for this satisfaction pushes itself into violence, whether it is war, gay bashing, rape (both male and female), and other horrors of exploding repression. When there is no Greenwood—no Sacred Grove—of desire to direct men into, the next available release is religious lunacy, and the kind of generalized state of war in which we find ourselves now.

This is not simply a question of "civilization" (and the corporate state) overcoming adolescent fantasies of male bonding and wildness, but a question of "How do you become the person you really *are*?"

I have been trying hard to answer that important question in this book, and certainly in the next several chapters. And by the end of *The Manly Pursuit of Desire and Love*, I hope you have the answer yourself.

Questions for You

Have you ever felt yourself in this Sacred Grove of Desire, the place where you felt most free and yourself? When did it happen, and where? If it has not happened, how can you imagine yourself getting there?

---

45 The Trumpet Call of Bisexual Desire

"Is it so terrible for a man to want more youth, more pleasure?"

The Hours, Michael Cunningham.

A lot of attention has been paid lately to bisexuals, mostly because of the fact that they seem to be missing in the sexual puzzle. They *exist,* and their numbers, according to various polls that have been taken, are either equal to the number of people who identify as gay or lesbian, or are much greater. But because bisexuals as a group do not come out in large numbers, their actual faces are rarely seen. You might find them more at a P.T.A. meeting, say, than at a meeting at a local gay and lesbian center, even one that now includes initials like L.G.B.T. (Lesbian, Gay, Bisexual, Transgender) in its name. If any group were going to be habitués of the Sacred Grove of Desire, bisexuals would be, since this place of private and intense meetings should well suit men who normally might prefer to disappear into workaday life.

Part of this comes from the difficulty of defining *exactly* what bisexuality is, a difficulty that some bisexuals actually enjoy—they don't want to be *defined* that much—but it is a difficulty that has made it hard for the more "out" gay and lesbian community to recognize bisexuals and value them.

So questions about bisexual men usually run to these: Are they men who have equal sexual/emotional attractions to both sexes? Men who feel emotionally connected to women, but not tied to them sexually exclusively? Men who simply enjoy a hot "queer" release every now and then, without any major emotional bonding to other men? Or men who may be primarily gay, but find at a certain point in their lives an intense attraction to women that they want to explore?

Each of these groups seems like they should be in a distinct category, but this leads to another question: Is it possible that what we call "bisexuality" really covers an immense range of sexual and emotional responses; or, as Ron Suresha, a noted writer and anthologist on bisexuality, calls them, "micro-sexualities."

Suresha's basic feeling about bisexuality of any nature is simple: "You fall in love with a person, not a gender. Look at your desires honestly, and take stock of them. See how these change, and be honest about how these things change and where you're coming from."

Unfortunately, many gay men (and most straight women) distrust bisexuality in men. Part of this is that they don't understand that the intensity of bisexual feelings is just as great as the intensity of anyone's feelings. So, if you have strong romantic feelings toward a bisexual man, his feelings will either be returned or mirror yours, or not be returned and not mirror yours, just as any other gay man's feelings will. Bisexuality in women seems to be another issue: it is much more condoned, even encouraged often as part of a "swingers" culture, but, from a lesbian point of view it is also very problematic.

Therefore bisexual women often bond with each other.

This brings up another question about bisexuality: is it sequential, or simultaneous?

The answer is that it can be one, the other, or even both.

But many people entering relationships with bisexuals get hung up on this question, again because they are not listening to the feelings involved. You can be bisexual and have simultaneous affairs with men and women, or you can find yourself at some point gravitating toward one gender, without changing your identity. That is, just because you are a man who is primarily interested in men, does not mean that you are not bi. You still will have a sexual response to women, even though you may choose not to act on it.

If you are "out" as a bi man, often the assumption is that you are now more "gay" than bi. But the truth is that even though you may be going to gay bars and clubs, or cruising gay sites on the Internet, your sexual feelings toward women are still around, but simply have gone into what can be a closet of their own.

For many bi men compartmentalizing their lives becomes necessary. If they are relating sexually with men, they might not want to scare off gay men, and if they are relating to women, they don't want to scare them off either. It is a short way, unfortunately, from compartmentalizing to going even deeper into an emotional very dark closet and many bi men talk about this. They have also said that because of this, their bisexuality works only on opportunity. They are too scared to venture out on their own with their desires, but if the opportunity shows up, at a gym for instance, or a nightclub, or a bar that is not specifically gay, or any place they just "happen" into, they will respond to it cautiously.

Therefore their same-sex encounters may be characterized more as "opportunistic" than intentional. This has led many bi men to be seen as emotionally "passive," furtive, or cold: they feel they have to wait for sexual opportunities to be offered to them, instead of actively going after them.

One of the problems with this secretive approach is that when these men are found out, because of a sudden bust at a rest top, for instance, or any number of incidents that can happen in a bar, the results can be disastrous: wives and families are hurt. Friends who had no idea suddenly realize the person they thought they knew was an illusion.

One way to get around this if you realize you are bisexual, is to recognize that at some point coming up it's important for you to have "the talk" with your wife, female partner, or even male partner. The talk should be basically about emotional honesty, how *difficult* it is to attain it, but how *necessary* it is for any relationship.

You can start by saying, "I think it's time we really talked about our feelings, yours and mine. There are things that are hard for me to talk about, but I feel close enough to you to want to share them with you."

You don't have to share everything about your bisexual feelings with your wife or partner, male or female, but you should let them know these feelings are there, and that you have also, at some point, acted on them. Or, if you have not actually acted on them, how you feel about that, too. You might say: "I regret that I've never been able to act on them, but I never felt comfortable doing it."

At least this way the person you are talking with understands that you may act on them in the future, that is, to deal with this particular "regret" in your life. What is important for you to maintain in "the talk" is that your bisexuality does not change how you feel about her/him (or even them), and you hope that it will not change the way they feel about you.

As Ron Suresha says, "If you've been living a lie, that's the problem. Don't stay in the closet, not to yourself or your wife (or other 'significant other'). It does not serve any purpose; and this applies to men and women who are bisexual. Many women actually feel less threatened by their husbands going with a man than with a woman. What is important is that you are open, because *shit* comes out of left field. It is when you've kept everything hidden, that things become total bombs."

The bisexual question—that is, why are people bisexual, and what's wrong with it?—opens up other questions. Is 100% homosexuality real, or is it simply caused by "gynophobia," a fear of women and their bodies? Why is so much of gay culture, and mainstream culture, terrified of any form of feminization, or a lack of very specific sexual goals (usually involving orgasm) in men? You can go after women or go after men, but if you go after both there is something suspicious about you. For thousands of years women have been known to be much more open to pleasure from other women than men have been seen to be open to pleasure from other men, and in a world that is very much male dominated this has placed women in a position of inferiority and distrust.

A lot of this has had to do with the power (and very fragile temperament) of that "thing" called the male erection. Most men are scared to death of their erection and what it can or cannot do. They need to be able to control it. There are times when you want it to pop up (with a bang!) and times when you have to work rigorously to keep it down (as in, "OK, boy, now let's think about income taxes, macaroni-and-cheese, and the Republican National Committee!"). Bisexuality brings up all sorts of insecurities about erections. One of the stereotypes of bisexuals is that they will fuck anything. Other lies are that they incapable of commitment, they will leave you for whatever comes along that is hotter, and that they are incapable of anything other than fence sitting.

None of these stereotypes and lies takes into account going into that place of intensely deep desires where erections originate. Men who are bi don't live in that place anymore than homosexuals or heterosexuals, but they are capable of accessing it with people of both genders, and some bi men are so much less gender focused that they go after hot "chicks with dicks" (male to female transsexuals who have kept their original male parts), or handsome female to male transsexuals who have kept their "original plumbing" female parts.

On the other hand, some extremely homophobic straight men find bi men more "trustable" than gay men. The fact that bi men are also with women simply makes them more kosher—they are then the *ultimate* swingers—and for years rock stars like Mick Jagger have proclaimed their bisexuality without losing a single fan. This brought out the idea of "style bi's," who are basically cousins to Metrosexuals, that is hyper-groomed straight men who skate cautiously around queerness without falling into it; or the "bi-curious," guys who hold on to their own hetero-sexuality and all of its securities of old-school family ties, while giving the eye to a "gay lifestyle" (meaning: good-looking gents who may be sexually somewhat fluid) that they find attractive.

Coming up with yet another hand, many bisexual men who identify and live very much in a mainstream "straight" environment have a terrible fear of what they perceive is the "gay culture," which they feel has all the depth of a Calvin Klein ad: "gay culture" is now synonymous to a lot of people with the consumer culture that says that all feelings, looks, and attitudes can be bought at a department store counter. Kids buy into this stereotype seriously, often to their own detriment, but if you are a man in what feels like a closet all your own, and who inwardly very much distrusts his own sexual feelings, what now passes as "gay culture" comes off as a real slap in the face to you.

You often find this attitude on the Web in personal cruising ads where bi men say, "No gays." They are not denying that gay sex is a part of the bi spectrum, but they are saying "No!" to a perceived stereotype that is as harmful as an immediate negative reaction toward bi men.

This brings up the possibility of bisexual men bonding with each other, and sometimes they do, but the question then is, how do they find each other, and also if the bond becomes really intense, are they still *bi*?

Many men have come out as "gay" after having a substantially bi, often suburban, passingly "straight" married history, when they finally realized that the intensity of their bisexuality was leading them away from heterosexuality. On the other hand, a lot of deeply closeted men never even have a bisexual bridge between themselves and homosexuality: once they come out, it is blatantly, openly as "gay."

One phenomenon that seems to occur often with bisexual, predominately heterosexual men is that in order to keep the "bi" part of the equation going, it is more important to focus on sexual activities than on romance. Bi men enjoy the physical intensity and novelty of gay sex, but often say they are not interested in falling in love with another man, or even in prolonged affection with him. For this, they will return to their girlfriends or wives. Some gay men actually find this refreshing: they can have really hot sex with a bi guy, without the "strings attached" of romantic commitments.

They are genuine fuck buddies—and all of this seems to work beautifully, until you go down that slippery slope leading to inevitably sticky feelings. At this point, even the most non-committal arrangements can explode into something like this: "You just broke our date because your girlfriend wants to go shopping? Fuck off!"

These basic cold "fuck buddy" feelings, that can still become complicated enough to threaten bi relationships, very much differentiate closeted white connections from the "down low" situation of many black men. They will tell you that even on the "down low" they still have big, even romantic feelings for the guys in their lives, who are often also black and living the same life they are. In both white and black situations coming out of whatever closet they are in means disclosing something to their wives or girlfriends, and this is still very threatening to them. Not simply in that they may lose their female partners, but that it will mean a big change in the way they are seen in their own world. This perception may be wrong, but it's still large to them, and very threatening.

Something that can be helpful is joining a support group for other men like yourself, and they are found in many cities, usually within lesbian, gay, bisexual, and transgender community centers. Or for an even more protective situation, you might consider group therapy run by a bi-friendly therapist. http://www.bizone.org lists bi friendly therapists state by state.

Still, for many guys who are still seen as "straight," coming out of a bi closet in any way can be extremely threatening. They may be living in a totally "either/or" sexually-binary cultural world: meaning that by coming out they are not "bi" in any form, but are branded now as completely "queer." This is particularly true today because of health fears. Many women are terrified of contracting AIDS or other STDs from a bisexual partner, making bisexuals totally *bogeymen* in the heterosexual world. That has made life for these men genuinely horrible, since so many of them can get sexual satisfaction only from very anonymous sexual situations—bathhouses, porno bookstores, rest stops, etc.—opening them up even more to the threat of STDs.

If you are a bi man, and I hope that a lot of bisexual men will be reading this, here are some things you should be thinking about seriously.

At some point you should inform your major heterosexual relationship to the fact that you do have bisexual feelings. You don't have to tell her that you've acted on these feelings, but she should know that you *do* have them. Also, make it plain that this has not and *will* not change your feelings toward her. If you are a predominately gay man and you decide that you have feelings for women that you want to explore, you should do the same thing if you are involved with a same-sex relationship. Some gay men find that they have these feelings after watching straight porn, and realizing that they are looking at the women as much as the men. Some gay couples find straight porn exciting, and get into bisexuality this way.

As Ron Suresha says, "Create the space inside yourself that is big enough to handle more than one relationship. Most people can barely handle a relationship with themselves much rather commit to a 'primary relationship' with another person. You need to become *big* to open up relationships."

This leads you very easily into *polyamory*, which I will discuss later.

Safe sex practices are extremely important to understand when you are connecting with people of both sexes. This means understanding STDs which are communicable in gay sex, straight sex, or group sex (if you are into that). One of the great fears women who are involved with bi men have is their fear of catching HIV or other STDs from a bi partner. Of course what they don't realize is that they can catch many of these same diseases from heterosexual sex as well.

Finally, in your Deeper Self, realize that there has been a bisexual component all the time. You are simply lifting the curtain on it, and there may be *other* curtains even beyond this one. But, as difficult as this may seem to you, it's very healthy.

46 Lifting the Curtain on Polyamorous Desires

"There is no one way that life must be,"
Oliver Wendell Holmes

As I said, mentioning the possibility of "other curtains," for some men it is a short trip from bisexual feelings to polyamorous ones. Polyamorous relationships are intimate, loving, and committed relationships with more than two people involved. Although polyamory is often seen in lgbt settings, with three men forming a committed threesome, or three women doing the same, it is also found among heterosexuals. Usually when this is done, it is triangle with two men relating sexually to one woman, but not to each other. The men know about one another, may be friends (or in many cases, not *good* friends, but simply cognizant of one another) but they are not in any way lovers as well. This does not mean though that polyamorous mix-gender relationships are always like this, and some "hipper" bi couples have gone after a third, of either sex and loved it.

(A note here: some men, but many more women, get introduced to bisexuality and then a more defined "gay" identity through polyamory. What starts out as a threesome among two men and a woman can end up being a couple with two men; or, as I said—and it is more common—a couple with two women. Again, because of the male more-focused erectile reaction, men simply focus their erectile response in a more defined way than women with their sexual response.)

Polyamory events, weekends, discussion groups, dances, and other events attract large crowds in larger cities, and it is possible to connect with other "polys" through the Internet. In fact, if you just key in "poly" on Google, "polyamorous" jumps right up.

Polyamory has a long history among gay men, and as I wrote in *The Manly Art of Seduction*, some very famous gay relationships have been polyamorous ones. The best example I know was the long-term threesome found among the writer Glenway Wescott, his partner Monroe Wheeler, and the younger photographer George Platt Lynes. This relationship lasted in its intensity for about seven years, but they continued to be close friends until Platt Lynes's death from lung cancer in 1955 at the age of 48.

I have known of gay polyamorous relationships that have lasted ten or twenty years, and they are also not strictly limited to young men, or even to two older men and a younger man. Often men in the later part of their lives, after they have achieved some economic success, realize that there is room in their lives for more than one relationship, and adding a third brings new interests and feelings to them.

Some men though are just terrified of this. The writer David Sedaris said in a piece in *The New Yorker*: "The reason I'm monogamous is that I'm scared to death of group sex."

I'm not sure why in his mind group sex is the only thing on the menu beside monogamy, and I hope his husband has the same feelings, because there is a big world going on out there and at some point in Dave's life a phantom desire to experience at least some of it may seductively crawl into his lap.

Thoughts for You

Have you ever had fantasies about polyamory? About having a threesome, or engaging in group sex? Have you ever acted on it? If not, what would your idea of a perfect threesome be?

_____

_____

_____

47 Cross-Dressing and Transgender Desires

For many gay and bisexual men male to female cross-dressing, aside from the wit and irony of drag-ball costuming, is a puzzle. The majority of these men are drawn toward masculine images and ideals; that is, they are drawn more toward the male polarity in what is perceived as a bi-polar gender system, than toward the female polarity. For this reason, a great number of male to female cross dressers are heterosexual.

This is also true about transgender men, that is, men who undergo surgical procedures to reassign their gender. The public often thinks of transgender men as male homosexuals who decide to become women, when, in fact, a large number of transgender men are heterosexual men who become female in gender. I say "gender" because we now see that *gender* is different from sex, and also sexual orientation. In fact, you can very much separate the three categories: there are men who very easily are taken to be "male" (that is, have all the male secondary sexual characteristics: heavy facial hair; deep voices; broad chests and shoulders; easily seen male sex organs) but who feel "female" inside. They would describe their inner identity as "feminine," but they are also very much heterosexual; that is, they are sexually drawn towards the opposite sex.

These men will tell you that inside they feel softer, receptive, more emotionally vulnerable, more caring, more drawn to a feminine world and role—even though from the outside no one would guess this.

These men often have extremely strong cross-dressing and even transgendered desires, while at the same time still being heterosexual. They don't desire men, but they desire to be "women." Often their sexual desires are fulfilled by women who understand hetero cross-dressing, and even enjoy their male partners engaging in it; or by "trannies," men who are either completely transgender or in the process. That is, they may have breasts and cocks at the same time. When these men do transition from a physical male body to a female one—that is, they undergo a complete sex-change—their partners remain women.

They were heterosexual before the operation, and they become in fact lesbians afterwards, because their sexual focus is still on women.

Straight men in this situation often find themselves real *outcasts*, especially if they come from conservative communities where even the idea of this is so attached to a despised and rejected "queerness" that their very lives are in danger. Often you will hear about some hetero man being attacked or even beaten to death, because they have been "mistaken" for being gay. The truth, usually completely hidden out of embarrassment, is that some cross-dressing element was also in the story.

I remember meeting some years ago in Reno, Nevada, a plumbing contractor who was cross-dressing. He was burley and heavy-shouldered with a pronounced 4 o'clock shadow on his face, but his desire to cross dress was tremendous. He had met a friend of mine who was gay, and decided that in Reno the only support he'd get was from the gay community, even though he himself was not gay. He ended up going into gay bars in Reno, wearing, I must admit, some pretty outlandish drag, because he could not go into straight bars. He said to my friend, "I guess now I'll have to learn how to give a good blow job."

My friend asked why?

"Because that's the only sex I'm going to get looking like this."

Speaking of which, there are in many cities people who advise cross-dressing men how to dress, put on make up, act, and speak as a woman. This is very important if you want to pass as a woman, doing what's referred to in the cross-dressing world as "stealth." That is, being able to pass so well that you don't cause any kind of comment or adverse reactions. You're simply taken for granted as being female in gender.

Many gay activists, several of whom have been friends of mine, have completely questioned the reality and politics of transgenderism. Their feeling is that if the complete spectrum of gender behavior and variations were allowed on a casual basis, without problems, men who once considered gender reassignment would not have to resort to it. They could be as feminine in appearance as they wanted to be, and the perception of them by others would contain no judgment. I don't buy this. I feel that there are men who feel genuinely female inside, just as there are women who feel genuinely male. Strangely enough, women who become male get much more support from both the mainstream and gay world than men who become women. Some of this may be a matter of ease in passing: we allow women to be much more masculinized than we allow men to be feminized. A masculine woman is "one of the guys," everybody's pal. A feminized man is seen as a eunuch, castrated, and powerless. He is seen as a deserter; he has deserted the various privileges and powers (real or not) of being a man—and a huge number of men hate this.

This does not stop female to male transsexuals from being harassed, and hurt by other people, of both genders, who feel threatened by any kind of gender variance; but I do know for certain that FTM transsexuals are very much welcomed into the gay world. Some of them make extremely hot guys—I know because I've been very attracted to some—while at the same time keeping a kind of feminine warmth inside that's beautifully emotionally attractive.

I have learned a lot from female to male transmen, and one of the things I have learned is that sexual orientation is permanent. Women who were attracted to men, that is, were heterosexual, usually after transitioning to the male gender remain attracted to men: they become basically gay men. And women who were lesbians remain attracted to women, and become, basically, heterosexual. However, there is also the question of awaking bisexuality here, or sexual fluidity. Once you have made a transition of this nature, all of your feelings and attractions may be opened. For some people this in itself might be scary as hell—especially in a culture that is working hard to close down desire. But the rewards could also be immensely fulfilling.

Thinking about the "scary as hell" feeling brought me back to another thought, which I'll talk about in the next chapter—what happens when genuine bigotry under the name of "academic freedom" rules the conversation?

More thoughts for you:

Did this discussion about transgenderism and desire open up some feelings for you that were new? Were they interesting, or simply scary?

_____

_____

_____

48 A Permanent "Niggerdom" of Desire

"If I had the power to do so, I would wish
homosexuality off the face of this earth."
Joseph Epstein, *Harper's Magazine*, 1970

In one of the most inflammatory articles ever published in a main-stream American magazine, in *Harper's Magazine* (then edited by Midge Dector, who, with her husband Norman Podheretz, became one of the founders of the movement known as Neo-Conservativism), in 1970, Joseph Epstein, a prominent academic and critic, ended his long cover piece entitled "Homo/Hetero: The Struggle for Sexual Identity" with these words: "There is much my four sons can do in their lives that might cause me anguish, that might outrage me, that might make me ashamed of them and of myself as their father. But nothing they could ever do would make me sadder than if any of them were to become homosexual. For then I should know them condemned to a state of permanent niggerdom among men, their lives, whatever adjustment they might make to their condition, to be lived out as part of the pain of the earth."

Earlier in "Homo/Hetero," (in what he thought was a more charitable vein) Epstein admonished that he simply wished homosexuality might be wiped off the face of the earth, because ". . . I think it brings infinitely more pain than pleasure to those who are forced to live with it; because I think there is no resolution for this pain in our lifetime, only, for the majority of homosexuals, more pain and various degrees of exacerbating adjustment; and because, wholly selfishly, I find myself completely incapable of coming to terms with it."

In short, their total extinction would be infinitely better than being branded with this "permanent niggerdom" of . . . well, being gay.

Epstein's work became known as "the Harper's piece." It immediately inspired a demonstration of outrage at the Harper's office by the Gay Activists Alliance, an early gay rights group, as well as a circling of the wagons by Epstein's right-wing defenders like Dector, Hilton

Kramer, and William F. Buckley, Jr. who felt that American freedom of speech was now on trial by the "politically correct." The right wing could feel smugly satisfied with this, just as it bravely put on a show that homosexuals were part of the gelded bourgeois—in their exclusive roles as interior decorators and hair dressers—and therefore were enemies of the beer-slugging, hairy-chested working class that William F. Buckley (who resided in luxury on New York's super-expensive Upper East Side, lived off inherited money, and played the harpsichord) so vocally championed. On the First Amendment issue, it was safe to say that no gay activists of any sort would be given a platform like *Harper's*, or *Time* or any other major mainstream magazine for decades to come.

However, the idea of desire pushing you into a position of "permanent niggerdom" is really worth thinking about. We find this very true today as more and more resources are being pushed into "anti-porn" measures, and artists who work with any material regarded as "pedophilic" are threatened with jail time. (I always say that at this point, Lewis Carrol, who wrote *Alice in Wonderland* and liked to take pictures of small Victorian girls, often in the nude, had better watch his ass—"Alice" and her millions of readers and admirers will no longer save him.)

One important concept I would like to leave you with is that within any kind of "niggerdom," that is a position in society you are forced into by shame and fear, there dwells a genuine humanity under it pushing fiercely to come out. Any worker for human rights knows this. So grab on to this humanity yourself, and to the greater depth and knowledge that comes with it. Being rejected by others is not nearly as bad as rejecting yourself, or even worse, rejecting your own Deeper Self, something that even Joseph Epstein found out later on,

He is now, against his own nature, embarrassed by the "Harper piece," and has repeatedly refused to speak about it on record.

49

So, Who's a "Perv"?
Or Is Your Favorite Fetish on this List?

OK, after that brief interlude in the "niggerdom of desire," how pervy are you—really? We know, somewhere in you there is distinctly something to curl the hair of your Aunt Sadie and her mahjong club, or at least start Joseph Epstein fulminating again.

So fess up.

But just to make you feel a helluva lot better here is a list of (fairly) commonly accepted fetishes and activities—although it is by no means complete. I'm sure that somewhere out there, somebody is coming up with a whole new sexual activity or interest, and at the same time a Citizens Committee is banding together to march against it, with drums, banners, and flaming torches into the night.

One thing I have noticed is that one man's history is another man's fetish.

My first lover had lost a leg six weeks before we met; so, does that make me a follower of acrotomophilia (getting turned on by amputees)? I think not. But what it did do is make me aware that the world is a bigger place than I, at 19, realized, and there were gay men out there who were also amputees, and some of them were extremely hot. As was my first lover.

In this section I have a list of fetishes and activities, and my own commentaries after the definition. I hope you'll read them, and get something out of the idea that no matter what turns you on, there are ways to understand and if appropriate approach it.

Acrotomophilia

Getting turned on by amputees. See above note.

Actirasty

Getting turned on by the sun's rays—how common is this? Except among vampires, I thought it was pretty normal.

Agalmatophilia

Getting turned on by statues—like generations of gay men were in the Classical Art sections of museums, before really terrific gay porn hit the newsstands.

Anasteemaphilia

Getting turned on by a person of extreme stature, either giant or dwarf—a constant feature of *Lord of Ring* movies. More seriously though, this fetish can open up a lot of your own personal narrative: that you want to be turned on by a person of great size, or that you find a person of small size endearing and *really* hot. When I was younger, I found big men fantastic, and often strangely humble, realizing how clumsy they could be and how difficult it was for them to maneuver in tight places, like your bed for instance. On the other hand, small men have a miniature quality about them that makes many guys blushingly unnerved. They also often have exquisitely boyish genitals that drive their admirers crazy.

Apotemnophilia

Getting turned on by oneself as an amputee—not sure if Captain Hook was in this group. And for God's sake, don't try this at home.

Autogynephilia

Getting turned on by oneself [male only] in the form of a woman. As any kid who's ever stuck his dick between his legs knows, this can happen. There may also be a cross-dressing element here; I'm sure that some men (and boys) have found themselves hard as a rock inside a pair of panties, a bra, and a girdle. But perhaps this kind of dressing only delivers them to their own sacred grove of desire, where they are free to be themselves in any clothing.

Autoplushophilia

Getting turned on by oneself dressed as a giant cartoon-like stuffed animal—I was always partial to Donald Duck, but will settle for Mickey and Goofy, too.

Chasmophilia

Getting turned on by caverns, crevices, and valleys: I guess this was where all the hot action was in the Olden Days when guys walked around in bear skins, but there is something about being in a natural, but often inaccessible place that can immediately lead to thoughts of . . . whoopee! In the rampantly sexually-active 1970s in New York, several bars tried to simulate caves, dark warehouses, the backs of trucks, and other off-the-track environments as places for erotic frolic, so here we had urban chasmophilia.

Climacophilia

Getting turned on by falling down stairs. A completely new one on me, and I wouldn't make a habit of it because it can get reckless. Part of this fetish, though, can mean being turned on by any unexpected, violent sudden act—in other words, something that can loosen a lot of taboos and repressions, combined with the fact that gravity is taking you down: so you are now powerless against it. I wonder if a fetish for waterfalls is in the same category, and I'm a bit disappointed that I can't find a word for that. This goes with Katey Hepburn's famous line after she and Humphrey Bogart came close to being tossed over the Victoria Falls in *The African Queen*. "Never did I believe that any mere physical sensation could be so exciting!"

Coprophilia

Getting turned on by feces—not be confused with *coprophagia*, or plain ol'-fashioned shit-eating, which I've been told can do terrible things to your breath. Rumors that certain movie stars like Tyrone Power were into coprophagia have popped up repeatedly. Shocking, but never completely proven.

Ephebophilia

Getting turned on by older adolescents, approx. 15-19. When men do this to young men or boys, they are castigated, hunted down, and ruined. When men do this to girls, well . . . they used to become the center of attraction at bachelor parties.

Exhibitionism

Getting turned on by displaying one's sexual organs in public—if we were not such a Puritanical, dick-loathing culture, this would hardly be a problem. The fact that a man's equipment is now denigrated as his "junk" says excellent things about this particular fetish, and I will talk about "junk fears" later. In ancient Greece displaying one's privates in public was hardly frowned on. Now it can cause a riot, and ten years in prison.

Fetishism

This is the generic term for most of what we are talking about here. It specifically means getting turned on by objects that have been in physical contact with a desired person. Personally I feel that all of Hollywood, most of opera, and at least 90% of our celebrity-driven consumer culture is about this. But—it is easy to see that one man's fetish can be another man's normalcy, or idiocy.

Formicophilia

Getting turned on by insects. I'd never heard of this fetish. Is it secret spider worship? Or people who believe *cock*-roaches are hung? I discovered it is actually about the feeling of having insects crawl over you, their lightness of touch, and the tactile feel of them—especially of ants or some beetles. I can really see the attraction of this with butterflies—butterflies often have a sexual association—their beauty, lightness, and how they can transform any place or experience. Imagine a whole flock of them landing on your "junk," and you can understand what I mean.

Frotteurism

Getting turned on by touching a stranger surreptitiously in a crowded place. For many gay men, half the fun of living in New York and being on the subways was about this particular fetish. Poets wrote about it, and if/when people became drunk and turned honest, they relayed their own fav stories about it. On a fantasy level, frotteurism can lead to many great "scenes" replayed in your own bedroom or play station, which can turn into a nighttime subway car, a darkened movie theater, or the deep sleeping hold of a ship at war.

Gerontophilia

Getting turned on by the elderly—I guess this is anybody over . . . OK, I'll leave that up to the reader, but it has made many a dirty old man deliriously happy.

Hebephilia

I was wrong; this is not about an unnatural attraction to Jews, but to kids—meaning getting turned on by pubescent-aged children, approximately 11 to 14. We presently consider hebephilia to be a more digestible word than pedophilia, which has become a genuine hate category. However, adults have been playing with hebephilia scenes for generations, such as in secret parties where adult women dress up as school girls; or in Helmut Newton's extremely prized photographs of "Lolita"-esque sirens; as well as the utter suggestibility of sexy-kid ad campaigns like the old Abercrombie and Fitch catalogues from the late 1990s and early 2000s. Since a lot of people might get into trouble remembering being *hebes* themselves, I won't put my two cents in here. But it is sad to me that we deny the sexuality of children, and additionally, we deny kids the kind of unstructured play that once often resulted in erotic experimentation. I'm sure you know what I mean if you are old enough to remember playing "Doctor" yourself.

Hierophilia

Sexual attraction to religious or sacred objects. Part of this attraction comes from the power with which we imbue sacred objects, and their "sanctity" in our lives, but it also should extend to "priest play," a common form of sexual play where one man dresses as a priest and goes through the rituals of priesthood, like confession or communion, while another receives these "sacraments." The truth, though, is that many practicing priests can attest that sexual interest in them is highest when they are involved with the sacraments, and they were often flirted with or downright propositioned either in the confessional booth, or in the midst of some kind of religious ritual.

Katoptronophilia

Getting turned on by sex in front of mirrors—all those hotels with mirrors on the ceiling know what sells. Sex with mirrors is only a short step away from DIY selfie videos; the truth is that most people are fascinated by the idea of looking at themselves having sex, or looking at the object of their significant feelings from a different angle. In many ways, the desire to have threesomes or engage in group sex is a variation on this same fetish: to look at sex from a different, fresher point of view.

Knismolagnia

Getting turned on by being tickled. Having experienced this, all I can say is, why let other people have all the fun? Some people are so repressed and touch sensitive that even the idea of this is "perverse." Still, tickling can add a lot of color to your sexual palette. Once you give into it, tickling releases a lot of physical inhibitions as well as laughter, which has been found to be excellent for your health. People who laugh generously actually stay alive longer—maybe simply because they are not depressed.

Lithophilia

Getting turned on by stone and gravel. I'm not sure if this refers to walking barefoot over stones—which can be fun when they hit all the beautiful pressure points in your feet—or fucking on tombstones, but there has got to be some fun in this somewhere.

Masochism

Getting turned on by experiencing physical and psychological pain. I think we went into this on the chapter on S&M. Just remember that there is a difference between pain you agree to, and pain that is inflicted on you viciously.

Or, as one S&M master once told me: "That's not S&M. That's just *meanness.*"

Melissaphilia

Getting turned on by bees and wasps, especially by their stings. As someone who adores bees, I'm not sure how to deal with this—they are amazing creatures. Wasps are another story, and I can say that they are definitely not my cup of anything. However, bee venom, which is what does all the nastiness in a bee sting, contains a mild dose of both dopamine and noradrenaline, both very powerful brain hormones. Dopamine is a pleasure transmitter: when you feel happy, rewarded, or positive, your brain is releasing dopamine. Noradrenaline allows you to concentrate, as in when you're driving through traffic or in the midst of a mid-term final. So having a small "hit" of both drugs delivered by a bee . . . well, I can't knock it, though it's still a pretty specialized turn on. Also remember that some people are fatally allergic to bee and wasp venom, so if you feel that you want to experiment with this, tread carefully.

Nasolingus

Getting turned on by sucking on a person's nose. This makes complete sense to me since the bridge of the nose is a very sensitive part of the face, so why avoid it?

Nebulophilia

Getting turned on by fog. Having seen enough English "Sherlock Holmes" movies, I can attest that a lot of hot things can go on in cold fog. Or in the fog of steam rooms. If this fetish also refers to weather conditions themselves, it is much more common than believed—huge numbers of people are turned on by steamy weather, as well as cold weather. When younger, I had a friend who was hugely turned on by snow, and loved having sex in it. I have talked about my own sexual associations with the scent of swimming pool chlorine, and I'm sure that my readers have other weather or atmospheric triggers that do exciting things for them.

Necrophilia

Getting turned on by corpses. This has popped up often in literature: Heathcliff in *Wuthering Heights* exhumes Katherine's body and lies with it (and after it was a year underground—*puh-leeze!*), and dozens of hot young vampire TV series inject it into Pop culture, but the real attraction of necrophilia is the complete passivity of a desired object; in other words, the dead cannot object. Many S&M practices involve immobilizing the "bottom" (including "mummification," that is wrapping the "bottom" in yards of bandaging material or plastic wrap, being careful to avoid the nose or mouth) so you can do this with the living, too; so if necrophilia happens to be your "thing," you might want to try it with a living object pretending to be dead. It's a lot less messy, and is, for the most part, legal.

Objectophilia

Getting turned on by a particular object, distinct from fetishism. This one is new to me, but probably not to zillions of teenage boys who are turned on by cars, or New Yorkers who are turned on by apartments, or anyone at all who's turned on by money. Remember what Henry Kissinger said about power, that it's "the world's most powerful aphrodisiac"? So, whatever you feel is powerful *will* turn you on.

Partialism

Getting turned on by a body part other than the reproductive organs: e.g., calves, chests, etc. If this term also includes asses, or as the English say, "bums," then most people in our contemporary world are driven half nuts by Partialism. I am particularly partial to necks, shoulders, also hands, wrists, and that beautiful place inside the crook of the elbow. In *The Manly Art of Seduction* I talked about seduction techniques using other parts of the body besides the "dirty" ones (which shouldn't, by the way, actually *be* dirty) and I mentioned that horses like to "neck," that is, rub each other's necks. So, go ahead—be like a horse and neck. Just don't nag.

Pedophilia

Getting turned on by prepubescent children. This is where the rubber hits the road, and people start screaming and kicking. I believe childhood and children are very sacred—a feeling the Greeks had—and robbing any kid of a genuine childhood by injecting unequal adult sexual aggression and its resultant power into it is awful. But I also know that sexual feelings begin much earlier than eighteen, and kids themselves should be free to understand their own sexual natures. However, just saying this could get me tarred-and-feathered inside many localities, and/or cocktail parties.

Podophilia

Getting turned on by feet. This is an extremely popular and, finally, talked about fetish—there are groups, websites, and tons of porn currently devoted to it. But I feel few people actually understand the significance of podophilia, and it's psychological and emotional depths. To begin with, human feet themselves are exquisite things, one of Nature's marvels of engineering. That these beautiful structures keep us upright, walking, balanced, and can do amazing things from tiptoeing and ballet, to football—like, who wouldn't be impressed?

The soles of your feet have more nerve endings than any other part of your body except the head of your penis, or if you are a woman, your clitoris. Since antiquity bare feet have been a sign of submission, humility, and also the receiving of hospitality. In the Book of Genesis, Abraham washes the feet of the three angels who come to announce that Sarah, his wife, will bear him a son in his old age. In Exodus, God at the site of the burning bush commands Moses: "Take off your sandals, for the place where you are standing is holy ground." In ancient Greece and Rome, the feet of handsome young men and beautiful women were especially revered, and it was rare in art to see them covered. After the bourgeois upper middle classes took over the world, being barefoot became a sign of poverty and ignorance ("Barefoot and pregnant!") which meant that for many men, especially gay ones, being barefoot took on an special note of forbidden sexuality. In my high school in Savannah, Georgia, in the early 1960s, boys who wore loafers without socks were sent home. My principal was quoted as saying, "This is a sign of open sexual rebellion and I won't have it." I have often said that there are two kinds of people: those who love feet and liars. But, concurrently, there are two kinds of feet: those you will love, and those you can definitely do without. And I am sure that most of my readers can understand this.

Psellismophilia

Getting turned on by stuttering. This is an interesting interest, and it reminds me of the fetish that Samuel Delany has written about—that he is turned on by men who bite their fingernails down to the quick. I guess that once more it is being turned on by a revelation of vulnerability, allowing long repressed feelings to come out.

Psychrophilia

Getting turned on by being cold and watching others who are cold. I guess this refers to people who are turned on by goose pimples, shivering, and having the color drained from someone—so there is an S&M side to this, in that you are dealing with men (or women) in a submissive position. If this applies to water, I am completely for it. There is nothing like getting someone warm by snuggling up to them in cold water and I have enjoyed that most of my life.

Pteronphilia

Getting turned on by being tickled by *feathers*. I guess this is a refinement of knismolagnia, although feathers do provide an additional kick in that they are so light, and carry a breeze of their own, as opposed to being tickled, for example, by a comb being run over the naked soles of your feet or inside your armpits.

Pubephilia

Getting turned on by pubic hair. This is a delicious thing, especially if you remember a particular "crab ladder," the term for a thin trail of hair that ran from your navel to your pubes. As a kid, I was mesmerized by seeing "crab ladders" on men on the beach, giving me this inkling of what was ahead.

Pygophilia

Getting turned on by buttocks. See **Partialism**.

Sadism

Getting turned on by causing physical and psychological pain. You can draw your own conclusions here, especially after reading the chapter on BD/SM.

Savantophilia

Getting turned on by the cognitively impaired or developmentally delayed. Like pedophilia, this is an extremely volatile issue, but one which calls to be discussed and explored. We are finally starting to understand men who are developmentally challenged as being disabled, rather than being labeled simply "stupid," "slow," or "retarded." I have known men who were drawn to such guys because they felt that they were less sexually inhibited than "normal" men who have absorbed all of society's rules and taboos. What most of us don't understand is that like anyone, developmentally disabled people have the same feelings we all do: desires for love and closeness, and of course fears of being hurt, used, and embarrassed. I explored an example of savantophila in my short story "A Small Triumph," about Peter Brogan, a thirty-eight-year-old New York writer, who falls in love with Andrew Allister, an unusually handsome nineteen-year-old boy with Down syndrome. The story takes place in the mid-1980s, when life in New York was a little less pressured with high-money stakes; pre-cell phones and social media. It was published in *Serendipity, The Gay Times Book of New Stories* (2004), edited by Peter Burton, from GMP, Millivres Prowler. I was pleased that Peter Burton published it, because the controversy around its subject is still evident.

Stygiophilia

Getting turned on by thoughts of hellfire and damnation—province I'm sure of the late, for the most part completely unmissed Rev. Fred Phelps. For people who come from and/or have escaped from strict religious backgrounds, this, without a doubt, can be a powerful turn on.

Teleiophilia

Getting turned on by reproductive-aged adults—isn't this also called "normalcy"?

Teratophilia

Getting turned on by the congenitally deformed. This is a strange turn on, but I'm sure that it has kept many sets of conjoined twins happy. On the serious side, there are some people who are turned on by amputees—called acrotomophilia—and there are numerous porn sites devoted to this. Again, the forbiddenness of this, and the fact that there is also an added element of vulnerability and submission, must contribute to the attraction of the fetish. In my book of erotic short stories, *Works and Other "Smoky George" Stories (*Belhue Press, 1992*)*, I published "The Cold," about a sexual experience with a handsome man with a leg amputation who appears, in the middle of a snow storm, at a mountain cabin in Upstate New York. The story was originally published by *Advocate Men* in 1988; my editor there told me that some of the editorial staff of the magazine were "squeamish" about the subject material and told him, "This is too 'sick' for us." In truth, the amputee comes off beautifully sexy, very real, human and dignified. Maybe that was what they didn't like.

Titillagnia

Getting turned on by tickling other people—a very common turn on, as is being turned on by being tickled. I must confess, this is one of my own secret delights as I remember being really excited as a kid by being tickled. I don't know if all boys pop a boner in the throes of extreme gales of giggles, but I was one. Were you?

Transvestic Fetishism

Getting turned on by female garments touching the male's skin. This is an extremely common fetish, and many straight men have it. To the point that in nineteenth century Vienna, it was common for upper class military officers to wear silken lingerie under their own cotton "unmentionables." They would often get these "favors" from their girlfriends (then known as "mistresses") or in a pinch from their own wives. There are men who get off having a brassiere strapped to their chests, from panties and garter-belts, or wrapping a woman's silk scarf around their genitals. Tennessee Williams uses the later as a motif in his play *The Night of the Iguana*, when the shy, virginal Hannah Jelkes recounts the story of meeting a lonely man in Bangkok who on a private boat ride together into a moonlit lagoon (now that's *very* romantic) asks, in the dark, for her silk scarf which he uses to masturbate with.

Trichophilia

Getting turned on by hair, especially long hair. Trichophilia is a form of partialism, and some aspects of trichophilia are also found in pubephilia, in that trichophiliac people often have a hair specialty, whether it's pubic hair, chest hair, underarm hair, and of course head hair. Trichophilia was extremely common in the nineteenth century, when a woman's hair was often covered up, or demurely gathered in a bun. The term to "let your hair down" meant that a woman was allowing a man into her intimate life: she was unpinning her hair. This term gave way to a piece of early gay slang: when you were dropping hints that you might be queer, you were "dropping hair pins." You were deliberately showing an intimate, even dangerous, side of yourself.

Today I have noticed that trichophilia is often exhibited for a particular kind of hair, such as red hair, blonde hair, or jet-black hair, and of course the kind of guys who go with the hair. Extremely dark haired men are often prized for their dramatic chest hair, the ebony hair on their legs, butts, and pubes.

Urophilia

Getting turned on by urine, or urinating on others. In the gay world this is known as "water sports," and it's extremely common. It is less common among heteros or bisexuals, although becoming more so. I have known many guys into "golden showers," and for a while it was considered a great safe way to have fun with other men. There are men who like to drink urine, and there is some controversy about that: some people have asserted that it is not only safe, but even healthy, while many health experts have maintained that some diseases like cytomegalovirus (also known as human herpesvirus-5) can be transmitted this way.

Vorarephilia

Arousal to eating another person's body parts. "Vore," as it is called, is a fairly rare paraphilia, but its most popular form can be found in vampire fantasies—where you are taking in blood, and maybe a bit of human flesh as well. There are men, and women, who get off on this as well as the idea of "eating" genitals. So, if you have ever surrounded a guy's cock with ice cream and enjoyed eating it off, you are on the route to it. There have been extreme cases of vorarephilia, as in the case of Jeffrey Dahmer, a serial killer and sex offender known as "the Milwaukee Cannibal": A truly terrifying and ultimately sad story.

Voyeurism

Arousal to spying on others for sexual gratification. I think that if we incarcerated all the voyeurs in the world, there would be about forty people left—and anyone who's ever been on a New York City subway understands this. It is important though to understand that privacy is a right we all need and want, so if you are specifically into voyeurism, set up a "scene" where it becomes possible or permissible. Bath houses are great places for this, and some bars and clubs. There is now an industry of "amateur porn" that exploits voyeuristic desires, and it is easy to find locker room videos on the Web. However, anyone gay or straight who can say that he has gone into a locker room and *never* gave an eye to another man who wasn't looking . . . I'd call him a liar.

Xylophilia

Arousal to wood, or forest. I'm sure this fetish has given many an outdoors guy a lot of happiness, and I am one of those too. There is something about the smell of trees and green things that I find extremely exciting, and much of classic English literature like D.H. Lawrence's *Lady Chatterley's Lover* and E.M. Forster's *Maurice* utilizes outdoor settings as a route to sexual freedom and the removal of inhibitions. It is very interesting to me that a lot of men see the outdoors only as setting for "blood sports" like hunting, and the idea of seeing the woods as sexual—rather than a closed bedroom—would indeed repulse them.

The opposite of xylophilia is xylophobia, which is actually widely spread: an extreme fear of wooden objects (for instance popsicle sticks, wooden eating utensils, etc) as well as forests and the things in them, not only trees but insects, bats, etc.

Zoophilia

Getting turned on by animals, or simply enough, non-humans. I don't know if mythology comes in here, as in getting turned on by half-men, half-horse centaurs, a fantasy that thrilled me as a young man, but horse fantasies are extremely big among people all over the world. Zoophilia is also known as bestiality, and it is a crime in most of the U.S., left over I'm sure from our Puritan roots. The strange thing to me is that although animals are hardly protected in most of the U.S., sex with them is hardly condemned. When I lived in Louisiana in the early 1980s, a state that has one of the worst records for animal protection in the country, the Louisiana state legislature passed a special bill condemning any kind of "sex film" involving bestiality. So you could trap fur-bearing creatures in powerful, spring-powered traps armed with spear-like teeth so inhumane that often trapped animals would gnaw a leg off to release themselves, you just couldn't shoot a film with an animal in the cast. Although I'm not sure if cinematic zoophilia ever was a problem in Louisiana.

Hundreds of thousands of gay men though are very hot for "bears," burly, hairy guys, and having bear fantasies is a big turn on to them. So this last fetish has a lot more coinage than we think, and it also has an aspect of trichophilia in it.

Thoughts for You

Do any of these fetishes particularly appeal to you, or repulse you? Which ones are in the first category, and which ones are in the second?

_____

_____

_____

CHAPTER 50

Some Basic Understandings: 6 Things to Give Yourself Nobody Else Will

These are things that will certainly save your own life, and add to the life you have. They are part of the gorgeous field of desire I want you all to have. Enjoy them, and if you can find something that I haven't mentioned here, give it to yourself as well. This means, think about it. I know some of these things are hard to realize, but the important point is to work on them often, maybe even every day.

The realization that you deserve love, for everything that you've been through, and certainly for all the work that you've done on yourself.

The genuine respect that you are entitled to: Never denigrate yourself. It does no one any good, least of all you. And it's basically a way of circumventing the very important responsibility you have toward your own accomplishments and gifts. In this sense, when others denigrate themselves, you easily see that they are doing this only to try to one-up you—to show that they can afford to be more "humble" than you. You don't need it.

An understanding of your own place in life: it's a large one, but not larger than it was meant to be. You have a place, and you need to claim it. When you do this, you will find that what you desire will start to come naturally.

A kindness towards your Deeper Self, no matter how you see this entity. How could you hurt *him*, this person inside you that knows you so well, that loves you and will forgive you? Getting closer to your Deeper Self is one of life's great accomplishments and gifts, and you are giving it to *you*.

An awareness of life's boundaries, and that as hard as they may seem, they are elastic enough to give you growth as well as limitations.

The permission to fail and still acknowledge the validity of your desires, as they make you into a bigger, stronger, and more loving and engaged person.

Thoughts for You

Have you made any notes about these ideas? Do they bring up long-held or long-avoided problems, or issue? Does bringing them up help to resolve these problems or issues?

_____

_____

_____

51

More Basic Understandings; 6 Things to Hold On to After They Mainstream Queer Life to the Point that It Bores You Shitless

1.

Only we understand our history; it is *secretive*—it's had to be—and very difficult for people to interpret and put into historical context. But only we can know and imagine what it was like to be queer in centuries past.

2.

We can still determine the boundaries and contours of our relationships, that friendships can have the intensity of marriage and our marriages can be based on genuine friendships.

3.

The warm authentic intimacy of our inner lives touching each other, with feelings of empathy, compassion, curiosity, and kindness are more important than mere acceptance.

4.

We can surprise ourselves with sparks of eroticism, playfulness, joyfulness, and exceptional "gay" delight.

5.

We can see deeper and understand in deeper terms what is going on than the general bland corporate culture wants to allow us to, or will ever admit.

6.

Men (and women) have a beauty in themselves that is beyond the material value given to them because of political and/or economic circumstances, and we need to stand up for this beauty, to speak for it.

52 Added Basics: 6 Foolproof Conversation Openers

CHAPTER

> "Modesty, for instance, may easily become a social vice, and to be continually apologizing for one's ignorance or stupidity is a grave injury to conversation."
>
> Oscar Wilde

Often what stands in the way of us achieving our desires is the fear of going into the unknown. And meeting new people is a perfect example of that—suddenly we clam up because we feel uncertain what to say, or even if what we have to say is worthwhile. We want to say something "cool," "interesting" or memorable. And instead what comes out sounds totally dorky and stupid.

But, please remember, it sounds that way only to you. In most instances the fact that *you* are actually opening the conversation is what's important. You are showing that you are interested in someone else, that you can extend yourself—and your own "comfort zone"— to include him, and, in fact, are presenting what a worthwhile person you are.

So to make things easier for you, here are six great openers. They are easy to remember, fairly simple, and the thing is just to keep one in your memory to bring out when it's necessary:

"Are you having a good time?"

"Are you finding things interesting?"

"What brought you here?"

"I noticed you when I first saw you. Where are you from?"

"Is this the first time you've been here?"

"I like your smile (or the way you look). What brings on a smile like that?

And, if things start to warm up:

"Is there something I can do to make things more interesting for you?"

You'll find that in all of these questions there are no right answers; the important thing is just showing that you have the energy and desire to start a conversation, and the interest in another person to pay attention to his answer. For more information on what to say and how to say it, please refer again to my book *The Manly Art of Seduction*, where I have complete scenarios for starters, middle conversations, and closings.

A note about having questions already in your mind:

Some of your may feel that this is contrived, or artificial. But it's a time-honored idea among people in public life. The Queen of England is famous for having four questions or statements for the throngs of people who come out to greet her: "Have you been waiting very long?" "How far did you come for this?" "Is this your first time here?"

And "How kind of you to be here."

So, if she can have a "pre-set," it's a good idea for you too. In the old days, questions often ran to "What sign are you?" which is really out of favor, and "What do you like to do in bed?" to which I usually answered: "Sleep." The essential thing about all conversation, especially now in our conversationally-challenged times, is that something is going on between two or even three people. The important thing is not to judge people on the content but on the intent. The intention being simply to open up a channel between you and someone else. Try to keep an open, clear mind about it, and once the channel has been opened, see what kind of interesting and pleasurable things can come from it.

Idea for You

Do you remember a great "ice-breaker" someone used with you, or you heard before? What made it good, would you use it?

_____

_____

_____

CHAPTER 53

Hot Fuck, Boyfriend, Lover, or Husband Material?

"I'd been eyeing Works, the foreman on the ranch outside of Modesto, all week. I'd been eyeing him and there were certain times he'd look at me and my knees went watery. He was tall and built like a cedar telephone pole—all muscle and fiber. Not bony, but beautiful, long muscles. It was the second evening we'd found ourselves stripped naked together."

"Works," from *Works and Other 'Smoky George' Stories,*
Perry Brass

One of the great questions a lot of men have is how to characterize someone they've just met—that is, what category is he going to fit in—and exactly how narrow should that category be? In other words, is he going to be a boyfriend, a hot fuck, a lover, or, better yet, real *husband* material? Sometimes this question is actually decided for us—your friends introduce you to a guy whom they feel is "perfect" for you. He is *prima facie* husband material. This is the guy *you* are going to marry, and they are sure of it.

The only problem is that although he looks fabulous, has a swell job, a beautiful home, loves dogs and children, is a Boy Scout and a church (or synagogue or temple) goer—basically, he's someone even your parents will flip for—there is not that basic spark of chemistry there. Nothing is going on sexually or even romantically.

So *what* do you do?

Then there's, again, the guy who's the perfect "boyfriend." He's someone you're going to date for a while, have comfy minor feelings for, maybe go to some events with—but you can't see yourself settling with. And, on the other hand, the guy who's so molten between the sheets, or on top of them, that you want to rip his underwear off with your teeth to get to what's beneath it.

He's the perfect "hot fuck," but there is such a stretch of empty space between his ears that it only becomes really painful and too obvious to you.

Again, so *what* do you do?

First I think you need to understand what couples are, and how do two men become a couple. (Or, if you are reading this and are a woman, and some of my readers *are* women, or a straight man, how two of *anyone* become a couple.)

Two people become a couple because they have developed a *culture* between the two of them. A "culture" is a group of shared feelings, experiences, ideas, attitudes, and reactions. You don't have to have a lot in common with anyone to have (or share) a culture with him—for instance, you probably know many men that you have huge numbers of things in common *with* that you wouldn't want to share a sandwich with, rather than a large portion of your life. With two men in the picture, you do have to develop a culture between you because there is still very little culture offered to you to share, even now in our fairly new Age of Gay Marriage.

With heterosexual, or mainstream, sexuality, a lot of this culture is already assumed: it is still assumed that a man and a woman will have a place with each other, will understand the place of sex in their relationship and it is assumed (to the misery, usually, of both of them) that the place for sex will shrink as the relationship develops, and other intimacies, such a children, come in. Also it is assumed that the continuation of their relationship is something that is good for society at large.

This is not true for gay men. Very few people, even at this date, believe that our relationships are good for the society at large—and if you don't believe that, ask any Catholic bishop.

So as gay men, or bi men, or men living within a regular situation that denies so many of their closest experiences, we have to develop this culture of understanding each other's feelings, of even reading each other's thoughts, and finishing each other's sentences. Often this is in an environment where for two men to be doing this is still in many quarters "suspect," leaving them open to rejection or actual harm. Even two men who are accepted as a couple will hear things coming from their friends and neighbors like, "You can tell *who* wears the pants in that house!" Or, "Don't be such a pansy, you don't have to give in to everything *he* wants."

I have friends in Bible Belt communities who still feel that many of their activities together can leave them open to confrontations, and physical or psychological harm. They still have to justify their life together: it is not a given with their families, co-workers, or neighbors.

They may have allies, but even their allies have boundaries into which *they* are not allowed.

So developing this culture is extremely important to coupledom. It can also bring in an atmosphere of security, and emotional satisfaction and richness that can be extremely sexually fulfilling, too. And it inevitably brings up the question: Can you develop any of this culture with the Hot Fuck, Boyfriend, or even Lover—developing, again, into genuine Husband material?

And conversely, can you bring your Husband into the (hotter) areas of these other relationship categories?

The answer is yes, depending upon your own flexibility, curiosity, and energy—and also your own boundaries, that is, the places where you find strength and security for yourself. A lot of men are frankly not capable of doing this, because they have bought into their own fears and internalized homophobia—the idea that sexual intimacy cannot go deeper than sex because it is about "queer sex." That alone makes it loaded with fears of exposure, pain, and even betrayal.

They're afraid that a "trick" will betray their own sexual secrets, and that investing such a guy with deeper feelings will betray long-concealed vulnerabilities. Unfortunately, this kind of reaction is often seen in sex party circuits, or leather and S&M situations, where you are following one sexual format—heavy but brief encounters—and another one, romantic love, seems unwelcome, if not unnecessary.

So how do you get over this, if that is what you want?

First by understanding how much trust you can place in a guy whose main attraction to you is that he does provide very hot sex. I understand what a conundrum this can present: sex is wonderful, but it can be misleading, as any congressman who's ever run after a younger polyscience major can tell you. However, sometimes your heart does comes between your balls and your brain, and that *can* be good if you allow it and enter the situation carefully, but with an idea that there is a possibility of trust involved.

A good example of this was found when the writer Samuel Delany met a homeless man named Dennis Rickett at a gay porno theater in the East Village in 1991. They had sex in the back rows, and Delany, one of the fathers of queer science fiction, was so taken with Dennis that he made a date to meet him later in the week at the same theater.

They started seeing each other at the theater, and Delany decided that he had to do something else, but how? Could he trust this man, who was homeless, in his apartment? He decided to rent a motel room instead, and spent the night there with him.

Afterward, Delany understood that he might be in love with Dennis, and repeated the motel rendezvous for several weeks, until he felt he could trust Dennis enough to take him home. Their relationship has been chronicled in a graphic memoir that Delany wrote with the artist Mia Wolff called *Bread and Wine: An Erotic Tale of New York* (2000); Rickett and Delany have been living together ever since. Their relationship is a beautiful parable for love transcending fear, with a vivid current of sexual arousal running through it. Being a great fan of Delany's writing, I have seen that one of the themes in it is that sexuality leaps over categories easier than a lot of other attributes, like money or talent. And it's sad that a more open, flaming sexuality of the past, in venues like porno theaters, bath houses, parks, and other places of sexual congress, which allowed a genuine democratization of sexual encounters, is disappearing. Too fast.

What this has meant is that we have too many couples who are as matched as book ends: both from the same economic, cultural, racial, and social backgrounds. Then they wonder why the hell they get bored with one another?

But hopefully this book—and the next chapter—will help with that.

Thoughts for You

Do you immediately put the men you meet into these categories, hot fuck, boyfriend, lover, or husband material? Has reading this chapter helped you change your feelings about this, or not?

_____

_____

_____

54 How to Put the Sizzle Back into a Luke Warm Relationship

"There is no one way that life must be,"
Oliver Wendell Holmes

One of the questions I am asked more than others is how do you re-heat a relationship that has gone stale, cold, or indifferent? I am asked this question by both straight and gay people—usually by straight women and gay men. I am rarely asked by straight men because they can rarely be that frank about their needs, which is one of the reasons why their relationships go stale to begin with. But here are some things to start the sizzle again:

First, learn not to censor yourself *or* your partner (or husband) about anything.

And I mean *anything*.

Any time you stick in a sex-negative remark, you are censoring him. This can include branding someone a "slut," saying that what others do is "wrong," not "politically correct," or dropping hints about how "sick" or "immature" they are. Any time you start off in this direction, you are pushing him (and yourself) to retract emotionally or sexually. On the other hand, *he* may be the person doing this, or he may simply tell you at some point that he is no longer interested in sex, of any kind, and the reasons for this can include:

He is too worn out from work. (When in fact he may be using work as an excuse *not* to be relating to you sexually.)

He finds sex repugnant due to his repressive religious background, or simply the past problems or dynamics of his family life. These problem can lead to a situation where in order to avoid a continuing, deep sexual intimacy with you, he will seek constant new sex partners, even though you are offering him the real emotional intimacy he wants.

He was sexually abused as a kid, and after an initial hot experience with you, his half-buried feelings about his past abuse have come roaring back, shutting you out.

He has erectile dysfunction problems, and so has become scared of anything to do with genital activities. In other words, as he may put it, he cannot "get it up," "follow through," or "complete the act," so he wants to abandon sex completely.

He is scared to admit that he is bored sexually, because he feels that to do so would label him "immature," "selfish," "shallow," or "sinful." So, at a certain point, after going through the "motions" sexually, he has finally quit even doing that.

Getting back to the censorship thing, if you realize that in the past you did censor him, set aside some time to apologize for it. Tell him that you did not mean to send a message to him that you felt sex was wrong, inappropriate, or should be limited only to things that *you* enjoy. Ask him what *he* enjoys, and tell him that you are open to hearing about it.

Ask him if he'd like to share his fantasies with you. Begin by sharing your own fantasies with him—what kind of men turn you on, what you'd like to do that you don't normally do with him, and feelings that you've been hiding. Try to open up those secret places in your "house" that you've been keeping tightly locked but that you'd like to visit. Ask him if he'd like to visit them with you.

Become much more *physical* with each other. A lot of men in long-term relationships start, as I call it, to "abdicate their bodies." They stop all forms of exercise and other physical activities that re-awaken them to their own bodies. "Real life" is now limited to the TV set or the computer screen. They binge eat because that gives them the only physical pleasure and/or emotional satisfaction they allow themselves. This in turn packs on weight, so they become self-conscious and ashamed of their own physical selves. They become turned off to the pleasures of their bodies—to the sheer physical release of exertion, of being spontaneous, being outdoors, being unclothed whenever possible, and getting sexually excited. They have allowed themselves to swallow the bilge of *something* being "inappropriate" about any one or all of these activities.

So it's time for you to initiate the change: to see that the body *itself* is pleasurable. You can be conscious of this and allow him to be part of this feeling and pleasure.

Go on private walks together, hike together, have time together doing something other than watching TV, eating in noisy restaurants, or being with other people and putting on a show for them of "togetherness."

Also, work to bring back the healthy aggressiveness of sexuality. We want to preserve a constant, cloyingly sweet, Hallmark-greeting-card aura about sexuality, especially in a long-term relationship environment. One of the secrets of sexuality is that the same hormones that trigger aggression, anger, and other immediate physical reactions, also trigger many sexual ones. These hormonal messages are also colored by other feelings, such as sight, smell, and touch cues (also known as the things and stuff that really turn us on), as well as empathy, emotional revelations, and plain unvarnished physical closeness.

So there is something wonderful about the surprise of "ripping" his clothes off (OK, you don't have to *actually* do that, but make him feel that you are), or suddenly feeling him up in the car, or at the movies in the dark. Actions like these can ignite some very cold relationships.

Also, getting out of your normal environment can switch on all sorts of responses, although sometimes trips are so stressful that the opposite effect happens. If this does happen, then it is very possible to *use* conflicts to bring about sexual heat as well. Some men find fighting itself sexually exciting, because the frankness of it turns them on.

But if you are one of these men, realize that these kinds of fights do not settle anything, and too much of this can produce so much tension in your relationship that it can end it. So, use stress *sparingly*, but be aware that travel stress can actually work to warm up some cold situations, if you don't use the stress to blame your partner for things falling apart or being disappointing. (And, in travel as well as other life adventures, something is always going to go wrong, leading to that classic situation known in the military as SNAFU: *Situation Normal, All Fucked UP.*)

So share with him your frustration, your anger, and that you're pissed-off at the airlines, hotel, cruise ship line, etc. But just make sure that he feels that he is the one thing making this holiday worthwhile and without him it wasn't worth doing.

In overcoming the coldness that settles into a relationship, you may have to fight his repressiveness to do it, and your own repressiveness as well. Our society is still extremely homophobic, and these homophobic messages seep into us all the time—I talked more about this in Chapter Eleven: Surviving Homophobic Poisoning. These messages in themselves destroy spontaneous, healthy sexual feelings, and in the past when gay men had to hide every aspect of themselves from most of their friends, families, and working lives, they made either the possibility of good, lasting relationships almost impossible, or forced them into an often tragic state of constant, emotionally damaging secrecy.

(I think it's very important for gay men of any age to understand this, and for those of us who are in the "double bind" of being gay and also a member of a racial or cultural minority to understand it even more. This goes *ditto* for guys who are involved with these men.)

Plan B

If, at this point, he brings up and asserts his own continuing sexual problems and feelings of inadequacy about them or doesn't even want to venture into them, it's time then to go on to Plan B.

Revert to what I call "Pre-Sex." Even if at one point you had a roaringly good sex life, Plan B is not about pushing sex in his face. This is not the time to unzip him in the car, or to make a pass at him while out on a nature hike. You want to spend time with him alone, in a comfortable, sexually-neutral way that allows *him* to warm up to *you*.

Give him a lot of attention, compliment him on the way he looks and that you like being with him, and show him that you are now open to him, but are not demanding that he respond to you. In a chapter in *The Manly Art of Seduction* on erectile dysfunction, I discussed a useful technique called "sensate focus," in which you spend a lot of pleasurable physical time with each other that does not involve genital touching. You are showing that sexuality can include other parts of his body besides the one in the groin area, since for many men this is a problematic region that opens up eons of pain and conflicts from their past and even present lives.

Once your partner realizes how warm, beautiful, and trusting this exploration of other areas of focus can be, he may start reacting genitally, too. In other words, he may become naturally excited, erect, and ready for a more involved sexual experience. I say *may*, because sensate focus does not work all the time, and he may actually have problems with real physiological sources requiring help from a urologist, or a neurologist, who, unfortunately, may not even be able to change the situation either.

When this happens, as part of Plan B, you should realize that some relationships simply may settle into a non-genitally intimate pattern. In other words, both of your dicks, and the satisfaction stemming from those parts of your bodies, just may not be involved. He may also be enforcing a psychological problem that is too terrifying for him to resolve: he has failed too many times in the past. And he is now too used to his feelings of inadequacy and shame to change them.

Your partner may find some fleeting relief from these feelings through quick anonymous or history-less sex (often in the form of phone sex, Internet site sex, or even sex with hustlers). But as a person who has such an extensive history with him, you will only remind him of his problems. This is a difficult burden for you to carry, and some men simply drop out of it.

But others find that on a real basis, the effort is worth it. They still find a lot of satisfaction in other aspects of the relationship, and they want to keep it going. Also, situations like this can allow them a certain amount of freedom, too. So, if you're exhausted from constantly trying to sustain, create, or improve a sexual situation that is just not happening, then it may be time for you, too, to look elsewhere for sexual satisfaction.

Plan C: Other Men

You can also go into "Plan C." Bringing in another man.

Many long-term gay (and straight or bisexual, for that matter) relationships have worked beautifully with threesomes. These kind of arrangements are getting much more prevalent although mainstream society, including the mainstream queer one, still has some taboos around them. Like I said before, David Sedaris has stated that the reason he is in a monogamous relationship is because, "I am terrified of group sex." I am not at all sure why his only alternative to monogamy is group sex, but allowing a third man into your bed and/or life can ignite a lot of sparks. Or fizzle out completely and even destroy what you already have going, if you do it without much thought, feelings, and sensitivity both to your partner and the third guy.

Although we are now in the Age of Gay Marriage, the idea that monogamy does not have to be for life is seeping into society through many directions (or orifices, to continue this metaphor). First, everyone's break up rate is through the roof—straight and gay—and often the only thing that keeps many couples together is pure real estate: it's too financially difficult to break up or live alone. We also have job pressures that are emotionally shredding, although these same job pressures are driving many people toward a coupleness that, in truth, they may not even want.

I have already written about polyamory, but simply as a wonderfully tonic solution to sexual boredom, a couple relationship that allows another person into it, if done right, can be just what the doctor ordered—especially if the doctor is realistic. Recently, Dan Savage, one of the most read relationship advisors in America, has come out with the idea of "non-monogamy" as a way of actually strengthening a relationship. I anticipated this idea by a decade in my book *How To Survive Your Own Gay Life*, from 1999, when I endorsed the idea of having an affair or extra-relationship relationship to keep a lot of pressure off an older, primary relationship.

I know of several couples who are now fairly formalized as threesomes: they sleep together, spend time together, and even live together. For two older men who've been together "forever," this can add a lot of fresh juice, insight, and excitement to their lives, especially if the third man is younger—and by younger I don't mean 20 or 30 years younger—but even, say, 10 years younger can still add a refreshing dose of new perspective. Also, it can help with expenses, chores, and keeping those nut-shriveling ruts from getting deeper and deeper.

Several years ago I met a gay couple who were in their eighties and mid-sixties. They had been together for almost forty years, from the time when the younger man was in his mid-twenties. They decided to invite in a man who was in his mid-fifties—mostly to play with the partner in his sixties. It worked beautifully. Both of them were financially well set up, lived in a beautiful, large house in the woody Connecticut suburbs, and were open to the idea of having "company."

Later, after the older man died, the two younger men continued as a couple. I think this is an excellent solution for many gay men who are faced with aging, but it could work just as well with bi or even straight couples.

In summary, how to restart the flames? Add more oxygen in the form of tenderness, kindness, and a very healthy dose of imagination. And realize that you have a lot less to be afraid of than you think you have.

55 The Desire for Non-Romantic Sex

"The world and man are not here to be improved,
but to become themselves."
Friedrich Nietzsche, *Thus Spake Zarathustra*

In our age of same-sex "till death do us part" marriage, non-romantic sex has become completely suspect. A lot of younger gay men don't even want to admit that it goes on, even while cruising compulsively on Grindr and other Internet meet-up sites. Part of this denial of non-romantic sex is our own heightened fear of strangers, something I spoke a lot about in both *How to Survive Your Own Gay Life* and also in *The Manly Art of Seduction*. Although statistically the overwhelming percentage of murders and violence occur between people who actually know one another, strangers have acquired such a threatening aura that even approaching one now propels you automatically onto what feels like a path of the most sinister consequences.

Part of this comes from the fact that our now mostly-digitalized lives have prepared the majority of young people with few of the social skills necessary for developing satisfying, spur-of-the-moment encounters or relations with strangers. These relations in the past were paved by time-honored rituals of etiquette that allowed you to open up a conversation with a person you didn't know, enquire how he was. Nod. Smile. Shake his hand—and, if things got off the ground, allow you to get his phone number.

Sometimes you didn't even have to do the smiling, nodding, and shaking, as there were places to simply get it on. Most of these have been closed down by skyrocketing real estate prices (yesterday's grubby sex club is today's high end Tuscan *ristorante*), health fears, and also peer pressure. Now that so many young people make most of their friends at work, there is no way that you would want *them* to know that you get down and dirty with strangers.

But the desire to have sex with strangers still exists, as it has for millennia, both with men and with women. Some of the earliest writing about sex has dealt it—from the Bible which records these instant fixes of sexual attraction, to the *Arabian Nights* stories and Chaucer's *Canterbury Tales*. Albert Einstein yearned for it, and wrote about desiring *"sex ohne hochseit"*—sex without marriage—which was as close as he was going to come to it.

The question is: how to satisfy this "itch"? First of all, don't beat up on yourself for desiring it. Understand that a huge amount of sexual fantasy does revolve around attractions to people we don't know, and it also revolves around instant sexual gratification without having to go through the usual formats of finding stuff in common like politics, sports, movies, and pop music.

The only thing you have in common is that you *both* want to do it. Right now.

It also means that you don't have to fall in love to do it. But you shouldn't count out the possibility of deeper feelings emerging from non-romantic sex, even if a lot of guys automatically discount these encounters that later become the fuel and substance for much of their fantasies. This is a mistake. They devalue non-romantic sex just as they are spending so much of their time and energy pursuing it. I've always thought that men like this basically devalue themselves: if your time and energy is important to you, then why shouldn't you be open to anything important that can come from it, even if it doesn't come with the usual respectable pedigree? So, you didn't meet each other at a Church of England high tea. You met on the street or the subway (if you were lucky enough), or at a bathhouse (if any are still open in your area and haven't been turned into Ikea parking lots), or a sex party. What's important is that you are open to some romantic feelings that come out of non-romantic sex, and hopefully he may be as well.

But unfortunately, you can't always count on that. One of the drawbacks of non-romantic sex is that when things do get "sticky," either on your side or his, for many men there is still that stigma attached to hot meetings that cooler, more socially respectable ones don't have. For one thing, it's hard to explain the meeting to your friends, or the society pages of the *Times* if you decide to get married. But the other thing is that in our age of Designer Living, where the term "luxury" is now applied to everything from pickles to toilet paper, these relationships based on steamy, hot sex seem "cheap."

This is a terrible mistake. There's a reality to sexual attraction and how deep it can go, and also how much deeper we can allow ourselves to be with it. This is one of the main problems with same-sex marriage. As much as we want it to take us to levels of commitment and depth we've never been, guys who are great marriage material are often, also, *not* concurrently great sexual material. They may be great at a cocktail party or with your Aunt Bertha, but misery between the sheets. This creates a huge conflict and often destroys a lot of happiness. We need those guys I call the "holy tricks," the sheer embodiment of our sexual fantasies and fulfillments.

So don't feel that you can dispense with them all that easily.

Ideas for You

Have you ever met someone on a more casual basis that you really wished you had turned into a more serious "thing"?

_____

_____

_____

Has this chapter helped you see that this is possible?

_____

_____

_____

CHAPTER 56 Arranging for Hot Sex in a Cold Time

"Remember to find meaningful and deep relationships in your life—either with friends or lovers—to maintain the depth of feeling that will round out your life. You will be a better person for it."

Jake Walker, Escort, quoted in
The Male Escort's Handbook by Aaron Lawrence

Besides using apps like Grindr, there are other methods you can use. I mentioned sex parties earlier. In many larger cities, sex parties, or what we used to call "orgies," were a part of the landscape of civilized urban life. (They also took root in some suburban and even country settings.) I remember a party in New York on the West Side that continued on Sunday afternoons for more than 20 years. It started in the late 1950s and went on until the mid-1970s, hosted by the same gentleman who made sure his apartment was set up for sex, with lots of clean sheets all over the furniture, gallons of lube, beer, and soft drinks. He did nothing to promote the parties (which he called his "Sunday after-church orgies"), but word of mouth spread about them, and he charged a minimal "donation" which eventually paid most of his rent.

Many of his attendees were men who were married, heterosexually, in the suburbs; it was also thoroughly biracial at a time when most bars were not. A younger man I know in New York, who goes by the blog name of "Orgy Guy," has done something similar. His name is Drake, and he's moved his party several times.

I asked him once what he got out of holding sex parties, and he told me, "I simply like holding orgies. There's something very cool about doing something that most people fantasize about, but don't have the balls to do. Actually, it takes a lot of skill to do this. I had no idea when I first started out what all this entailed. Like getting the word out, dealing with the competition, and also learning how to deal with guys who fuck up things—like they just add a bad vibe to what's going on. They don't want to play, or they stand around and smirk, or they get really pissed because nothing's happening that excites them. I have had to tell several guys not to come back. Usually, what I tell them is 'This may not be the party for you.' They get that. But you have to learn to deal with a lot."

You certainly might not want to go as far as holding sex parties of your own, but what I'm saying about this avenue and venue of meeting and sexual expression is that people should be a lot more open to them, and also respectful of them. And of the guys who run them. In New York there used to be an underground of sex party arrangers who knew each other and tried to respect each other's turf. Some parties specialized in men of a certain age, racial background, or size, and others were more open to everyone—although many older men I knew complained about being discriminated against in these more "open" parties. So, basically, like a lot of society, they were only "open" to some.

Actually, one of the most democratic of all is the New York Jacks (http://www.nyjacks.com), which still meets after more than twenty years. It is a masturbation only "club" (you can join it to get a discount on their reasonable party entry fees), and any male, regardless of size, race, age, sexual preference and/or orientation, and even physical disability can enter a party. There is something Whitmanesque about this "democratic vista" of male sexuality, of "adhesion," as Whitman called it, when men gathered together to celebrate their closeness and fondness for each other despite all the barriers that would keep them apart.

Going "Professional"

For many men seeking hot sex at any time, going to an escort or rent-boy service is the thing to do. Anyone who has ever been "in the life" will tell you that in this world, you do get what you pay for—and hopefully nothing that you don't pay for (as in STDs, or violence). Going to professionals has now become much easier, more secure, and trustable through the Internet. Some sites like Men4Men even give ratings from past customers, and you can find out if your prospective Pro takes credit cards, what his hours are, what he will do (and not do), and what other kinds of services are included, such as massage, weekend escort, or even long term companionship.

In our time of affluence when lots of men have more money than time—and they know exactly what they want—going to rent boys makes a lot of sense, and some pros understand exactly what "kinks" work for what clients, how far to take things, and exactly where to put that needed "happy ending."

Some things to understand:

Just because he's charging you, and is a "pro," does not mean that you can demean, insult, or hurt him. He has feelings, too, just like you. So if you think your money allows you to be an asshole, forget it. Since most pros, especially nowadays, desire repeat business, he will also not be out to demean, insult, or hurt you.

A lot of extremely successful men have taken on and kept younger guys (and some of them have done the same to older men, too). So it's possible to meet the "man of your dreams" who can accept checks. Not usual, but not impossible, either. It all depends on how open you are, and realistic. If the use of money is involved, expect that it will be a part of the relationship: it is what brought you together, and it can keep you together. Many "socially successful," beautiful women understand this, and so do "socially successful," handsome men. Therefore, if you are open to having a longer-term relationship with a pro, don't expect him to "fall in love with you" and money will no longer be a part of the equation between you. It was there at the beginning, and it will have to stay there.

Safe sex is very important in situations with professionals—so don't think you can bareback, just because you're paying him. (However, if he does offer this, I would definitely turn him down.) Safe sex is important for you, and for him. Interestingly enough, the incident of AIDS among sex-workers is no higher than the general population in the US (it may be higher elsewhere). So these men want to stay healthy, and it should be important for you to help in that.

Now because of the Internet, male sex-workers are not there to shake you down, and any rate you agree upon sticks. This means you can budget exactly what you need to spend, and then decide how far you want to go with your money. If you want to see him again, in the near future, what this will mean to you financially. Some men may work out a deal with you, and you can be open about that, too. But you're not there to bargain him down, just as he should not be there to try to get more money out of you.

57 Responsible Sexuality: Keeping Your Feelings Available and Yet Protected

> "There is no kindness of heart without a certain amount of imagination."
>
> Joseph Conrad, "Amy Foster"

Although we've been living in the Safe Sex Epoch for several decades, I feel that there's been very little talk about responsible sexuality—in other words, understanding that there is more to it than just using a rubber. First, let's frame this in some questions you need to ask yourself before entering a sexual situation, either with one other person, or several other people.

1. What do I want to get out of this situation, and what boundaries am I placing around myself that I feel I need to put in place for my own protection?

What you want to get out of the situation can be limited simply to "hot sex" and getting off, or it can include getting to know someone else on a physically intimate basis and establishing a level of affection and physical trust with that person. As I have said before, being sexually attracted to your friends, in an environment of mutual respect, is a wonderful thing. In my own generation, which came into adulthood in the late 1960s and through the 1980s, having "sexual friends" was very common. At this point, the whole idea is looked down upon horribly, which has added stress both to intimate relations (your husband who now must be "everything" to you) and to more casual ones (such as, in "accidentally" finding yourself attracted to friends—for some people, this is true disaster).

2. How far can I go, and still feel comfortable about what's going on?

For some people, this is a really hard question, but also a sign of maturity. You *do* want to stretch out of the boundaries of your social friends. You *do* want to get to know some men on more than just a quickie sex level, but there is always the fear that they may not be ready for this as well—and you don't want to be left feeling embarrassed and rejected.

If you are in this situation, let me assure you that the only mistake you'll be making is not realizing your own value. As I have talked about valor *and* value before, let me say, once again, that both only strengthen you. They are the hallmarks of genuine success in a human being: to have the strength, self-confidence, and self-worth to be able to extend yourself to others is one of the highest levels of achievement. I see around me everyday how much of this is lacking, and one of the main messages of my work has been to tell men how important it is to connect with this sense of strength and self-worth within yourself.

3. What can I do to make other men feel that I am worthy of their trust, respect, and love?"

First of all, show that you are genuinely interested in them, and not simply another narcissistic jerk. Frankly, a lot of men have to train themselves to do this. We live in such an insecure "Me First" culture where, on one hand, most men feel completely dismissed and forgotten—unless they are in some kind of magical aura of stardom and celebrity—and, on the other, where they have to constantly push themselves ahead of the game, that a lot of guys have not even learned how to ask the simple question:

"How are you?"

(Unfortunately, I still keep hearing crap like "What-up?" and "What's goin' on?" This is fine for infantile boys. But when you revert to this because you think it's cool—and your primary man-model is Jay-Z—you're effectively squashing any revelation of authentic feelings.)

So, show that you can extend yourself to men with genuine interest. But secondly, show that you are capable of a secure centeredness within yourself. You can ask how others are because you are secure enough to be interested: this is extremely attractive to other men. You are not falling all over them, but pulling them into your own genuine, beautiful centeredness.

Within that centeredness are your own spiritual feelings, private feelings, and the genuine history of yourself that has allowed you to develop into a capable person. It is that place where that important, balancing Deeper Self that loves you resides. The Deeper Self allows you to show that you are not a narcissistic jerk, but you are not inviting jerks, either. You don't have the time for them and time, in your life, is precious.

Therefore this sense of interest in others, caring, and maturity has to go both ways, but it can certainly begin with a more secure you.

4. How do I take care of myself when I've been hurt?

A very important question, and my answer is that you need to capture *your own innate courage* and extend it to yourself. Again, this means that you are capable of courage because you value yourself. Often courage has to rush in when other things, like reason, have been missing in other people. *You* need to provide this necessary sense of reason to avoid disaster (someone is drunk and at the wheel, for instance), or when you have been chosen by extremely trying circumstance (the kind we read about in the news all the time) to lift yourself out of despair.

But courage extended to yourself will make you realize that no matter how badly you've been hurt, you can face tomorrow, that you mean a lot more to people than you think (we all do, believe me!), and that at a certain point you can face him, no matter whoever he is, and yourself.

But facing *yourself* is the most important part of this equation.

It's also important to have the support of friends, and to realize, as I state plainly in *The Manly Art of Seduction*, never to *reject yourself.* Just the fact that you are reading this book means that you have a desire for, and a connection to, a greater depth within you that can sustain you and also bring others to you. You are developing curiosity, kindness, and valor towards others, just as you are developing it within your own Deeper Self, this beautiful inner *personhood* who has been with you your whole life and whose purpose is to love you.

You may personify him as God, Jesus, or someone who has been close to you in your past, but he does love you from within, and he will help you to heal and to be able to continue.

Questions for You

Do you feel that you've been hurt in the past, and that this hurt has kept you from developing other relationships? Has this chapter been helpful for you?

_____

_____

_____

58 The Desire to Stay Young, and for Young Men

People often say that "queer life" is completely youth oriented and age-ist. I disagree 100%. Ok, maybe not 100%, but at least 90%. It is youth oriented, and it is ageist, but no more so than mainstream American life which is based now on unrelenting, 200%, 24/7 competition: in other words, life is now a war—declared or undeclared—to survive in the "open market," and the young, as ever, are so much better at adapting to it than the old (or at least older, if you can't under any circumstances consider yourself "old").

Actually I feel that, currently, gay life is much less ageist than it was when I was a kid, just coming out into the world and sneaking into gay bars at the age of 17 or 18. Back then, when people were still us-ing cuneiform to write with, you were not allowed to age and be gay: you were supposed to be dead at least by 40. If you didn't kill yourself, someone else would do it. Men over 40 were terrified of being pigeon-holed as "homos," so in abject fear they clung to their "bachelor" youth as either a mask to hide behind or a desperate form of camouflage. The majority of gay bars were filled with what I used to call "the world's oldest college kids," men in their 40s and 50s still wearing varsity sweat shirts, trying to look blandly preppy and blend into a WASP Ivy-League culture in order to be perceived as "regular guys," or regular boys.

One of the most distinct memories I have from those days was meeting a handsome man at a gay coffee house in San Francisco in the mid-1960s who told me that, on the verge of his 29th birthday, he was considering suicide.

"It's all over after 30," he told me. "Nobody will look at you."

One of the delights of living today is encountering scores of men in middle age and older looking for other men in their age group. There is something incredibly hot about getting past all the consumer bullshit circling youth, and genuinely eroticizing your own generation: finding good-looking men at your own age level definitely *slurpable*.

This has meant that my generation, the unapologetic baby boomers, wants to keep their bodies fit and their minds open to new possibilities. I have seen this happening with much older men, some even approaching ninety—men who in past generations would only be thinking about where their burial plot was going to be located.

Now they are saying: "Screw that! Life's too much of an adventure to stay out of it."

I love this attitude of staying alive and young—and that many of us who are survivors of so much (as well as AIDS) have embraced it. I think it's an important feeling to impart to younger men too. But unfortunately I see a lot of younger men in our easily jaded, over-worked, media-saturated age who don't have it. As I have said before, they are too much the victims of the Culture of Rejection we live in. They have yet to understand that there is real work for us to do, what I referred to as the "gay work," and we can do it at any age. In *How to Survive Your Own Gay Life*, I talked about the importance of this work, and that we need *real* work to stay alive.

Here Is a Recap of that "Work"

We are a part of the actual balance of nature. Queer men in whatever guise or format they come in, have been around since the dawn of time. The very first recorded human narrative, the saga of *Gilgamesh*, deals with a passionate relationship between two men, Gilgamesh, the hero, and Enkidu, the wild man he discovers and tries to bring back to life after illness. Evidence of homoerotic activity has been around for thousands of years; it was often repressed and we are now finally coming to grips with it.

Men are beautiful—simple as that. As creatures of strength, pathos, valor, humor, vitality, and love, they—*we*—are beautiful. It is important to see that. Our worth is not just how much money we make, how willing we are to kill each other, or our ability to compete in a world that often discards yesterday's winner as well as losers.

We need to be able to tell our stories honestly and completely. This is often the role of gay men in society: to be a point of consciousness where and when "normal" men are scared of opening themselves up. We need to be able to tell our stories, and also listen to the stories of others and pay attention to them. Again, men have been brainwashed that any kind of attention paid to other men is "queer," and suspect. So that is definitely part of our work: to tell, and to listen.

Gay, bisexual, and trans people are the healers, builders, artists, and believers in a powerful Universe that we are especially in contact with. We are a part of the secret past as well as the wonderful future. We are allies of women, and very strong allies of other men, too.

It is part of our work to lead with our hearts. As I wrote in *How to Survive Your Own Gay Life*: "As part of the gay work, we preserve what has become a secret language of tenderness towards other men. Since women now try to speak as toughly as men, in heterosexual relationships this 'language of tenderness' towards men may be completely absent. Therefore, straight men rarely find themselves addressed in terms of privacy, warmth, and sensitivity, and many of them yearn for a return to these terms."

Although we live now in the amazing age of gay marriage, it is important for us to engage with and nurture other "queer" men as our friends—and also, whether openly or not, lovers, even if the love may not be overtly physical. Many men are now trying hard to keep a heterosexually-modeled monogamy within their often very public gay marriages. Monogamy is an important part of many relationships, and I believe that it can impart huge depth and closeness to them. But a monogamy that is imposed and enforced is artificial and frankly harmful. So I think it is part of the gay work to pull other gay or bisexual men into your life, to keep them from feeling isolated and apart, and to keep your own world view from becoming narrow and closed-in. I still believe in the joys of gay tribalism, and how this touching closeness with other men brings life and light to us.

Finally, to engage the Deeper Self with the rest of the world. This self that loves you, that is capable of love on a larger scale—don't hide it. But bring it out regularly. The Deeper Self is our own soul coming forth; it is part of our sexuality, and is at the heart of the rich grove of desire we long to find and to seek emotional, psychological, and spiritual nourishment in.

59 A Final Calling for Love and Desire

"There are certain physical qualities like lightness . . .
You have to have a lot of power to create that.
And the ability to go beyond yourself."
Gelsey Kirkland, former Balanchine dancer
with the New York City Ballet

You may have noticed that in this chapter I have reversed the title of the book, from "Desire and Love" to "Love and Desire." This was not an accident. What I wanted to do in this book was to open you up to a deeper calling from yourself to others. The calling would originate from your Deeper Self, and bring the world back to you—hopefully with the sexual and emotional satisfaction you want. To do so, you need both to open yourself up and let go of a lot of the pre-conditioning and baggage we all accumulate. One of the worst pieces of this baggage is everything you've been told you can't do, or shouldn't do, or can't even *think* about doing. While writing this book I had a lot of help from the people who've been so good to me, who have formed me as a person, and also from my own experiences, and, of course, those of others. Desire is still the dirty place in many people's hearts; the place they want to kick in the butt to make themselves clean. That is sad. Desire makes us vulnerable and in this time when privacy and genuine closeness are under siege, vulnerability is the last thing most people *desire*.

But by looking deeper into desire, and seeing exactly what it is and how it fits into the larger picture of yourself—the one you are really looking for—I want to strengthen you. I want you to be able to use desire, and seduction, to come out of your own shell, and enjoy the world.

To do so requires that some work must be done—whether you want to call this the "gay" work, or the "bi" work, or even the "regular" work of humans—in any case, this work is something that makes life worthwhile. This is a call for *genuine work*, which engages the

217

heart, the mind, and the body, and gives us a position to know what is valuable and what is not. It allows us to value ourselves, and that is the greatest desire I have for every one of you.

Perry Brass

Perry Brass

Originally from Savannah, Georgia, Perry Brass grew up, in the fifties and sixties, in equal parts Southern, Jewish, economically impoverished, and very much *gay*. To escape the South's violent homophobia, he hitchhiked at seventeen from Savannah to San Francisco—an adventure, he recalls, that was "like Mark Twain with drag queens." He has published nineteen books and been a finalist six times in three categories (poetry; gay science fiction and fantasy; spirituality and religion) for Lambda Literary Awards. His novel *Warlock* received a 2002 "Ippy" Award from Independent Press Magazine as Best Gay and Lesbian Book, as did his book *The Manly Art of Seduction*, in 2011. His novel *King of Angels* was a finalist for a prestigious Ferro-Grumley Award in 2013.

He has been involved in the gay movement since 1969, when he co-edited *Come Out!*, the world's first gay liberation newspaper. Later, in 1972, with two friends he started the Gay Men's Health Project Clinic, the first clinic for gay men on the East Coast, still surviving as New York's Callen-Lorde Community Health Center. In 1984, his play *Night Chills*, one of the first plays to deal with the AIDS crisis, won a Jane Chambers International Gay Playwriting Award. Brass's numerous collaborations with composers include the poetry for "All the Way Through Evening," a five-song cycle set by the late Chris DeBlasio; "The Angel Voices of Men" set by Ricky Ian Gordon, commissioned by the Dick Cable Fund for the New York City Gay Men's Chorus, which featured it on its *Gay Century Songbook* CD; "Three Brass Songs" set by Fred Hersch; "Five 'Russian' Lyrics," set by Christopher Berg, commissioned by Positive Music; and "Waltzes for Men," also commissioned by the DCF for the NYC Gay Men's Chorus, set by Craig Carnahan; "The Restless Yearning Towards My Self," set by opera composer Paula Kimper, commissioned by Downtown Music; and the song cycle "What We Did Not Know" set by composer Scott Gendel.

Perry Brass is an accomplished reader and voice on gender subjects, gay relationships, and the history and literature of the movement towards glbt equality. He has taught numerous workshops and classes in writing and publishing fiction, and the hidden roots of gay culture. He lives in the Riverdale section of "da Bronx," but can cross bridges to other parts of America without a passport.

About Cover Artist George Towne

Born in Pennsylvania and raised in Port Jervis, New York, George Towne realized he loved drawing as a young man, often copying caricatures out of old *Mad* Magazines. After his high school art teacher bought him his first set of oil paints, he became more serious about art, especially captivated by the works of Caravaggio, Velasquez and the American painter Thomas Eakins.

He came to New York City 20 years ago to attend the School of Visual Arts, where he earned both a B.F.A. and an M.F.A. His paintings have been featured in solo exhibitions at the Michael Mut Project Space in New York City; the Barbara Ann Levy Gallery; in Cherry Grove, Fire Island; and the Delaware Valley Arts Alliance, in Narrowsburg, New York. He has also been highlighted in several group shows, including recent ones in both the Wooster Street and Prince Street spaces of the Leslie-Lohman Museum of Gay and Lesbian Art, at the Forbes Gallery on Fifth Avenue, and the National Arts Club on Gramercy Park.

His work has been reproduced and written up in *American Artist Magazine*, *Art & Understanding (A&U) Magazine*, *Time Out New York*, and *HX*. In the spring of 2010 *Next Magazine* featured a George Towne piece on its cover. He has also been featured in the German publisher Bruno Gmunder's books *Stripped, Uncensored*; *Big Love;* and *Raunch*; and Schiffer Publication's *100 Artists of the Male Figure*, as well as Firehouse Studio Publication's *Powerfully Beautiful*.

Towne lives in New York's East Village, where he continues his love of painting, depicting masculine images as well as his love of landscape and other subjects. For more about his work: georgetowneart.com.

Other Books by Perry Brass

SEX-CHARGE

". . . poetry at its highest voltage . . ."

Marv. Shaw in *Bay Area Reporter*

Sex-charge. 76 pages. $6.95. With male photos by Joe Ziolkowski.
ISBN 0-9627123-0-2

MIRAGE

ELECTRIFYING SCIENCE FICTION

A gay science fiction classic! An original "coming out" and coming-of-age saga, set in a distant place where gay sexuality and romance is a norm, but with a life-or-death price on it. On the tribal planet Ki, two men have been promised to each other for a lifetime. But a savage attack and a blood-chilling murder break this promise and force them to seek another world, where imbalance and lies form Reality. This is the planet known as Earth, a world they will use and escape. Finalist, 1991 Lambda Literary Award for Gay Men's Science Fiction/Fantasy. This classic work of gay science fiction fantasy is now available in its new Tenth Anniversary Edition.

"Intelligent and intriguing." Bob Satuloff in *The New York Native*

Mirage, Tenth Anniversary Edition. 230 pages. $12.95.
ISBN 1-892149-02-8

CIRCLES

THE AMAZING SEQUEL TO *MIRAGE*

"The world Brass has created with *Mirage* and its sequel rivals, in complexity and wonder, such greats as C. S. Lewis and Ursula LeGuin."

Mandate Magazine, New York

Circles. 224 pages. $11.95.
ISBN 0-9627123-3-7

OUT THERE

STORIES OF PRIVATE DESIRES. HORROR. AND THE AFTERLIFE.
". . . we have come to associate [horror] with slick and trashy chiller-thrillers. Perry Brass is neither. He writes very well in an elegant and easy prose that carries the reader forward pleasurably. I found this selection to be excellent."

The **Gay Review**, Canada

Out There. 196 pages. $10.95.
ISBN 0-9627123-4-5

ALBERT

or *THE BOOK OF MAN*

Third in the *Mirage* trilogy. In 2025 the White Christian Party has taken over America. Albert, son of Enkidu and Greeland, must find the male Earth mate who will claim his heart and allow him to return to leadership on Ki.
"Brass gives us a book where lesser writers would have only a premise."

Men's Style, New York

"If you take away the plot, it has political underpinnings that are chillingly true. Brass has a genius for the future."

Science Fiction Galaxies, Columbus, OH

"Erotic suspense and action . . . a pleasurable read."

Screaming Hyena Review, Melbourne, Australia

Albert. 210 pages. $11.95.
ISBN 0-9627123-5-3

Works

AND OTHER "SMOKY GEORGE" STORIES, EXPANDED EDITION
"Classic Brass," these stories—many set in the long-gone seventies, when, as the author says, "Gay men cruised more and networked less"—have recharged gay erotica. This Expanded Edition contains a selection of Brass's steamy poems, as well as his essay "Maybe We Should Keep the 'Porn' in Pornography."

Works. 184 pages. $9.95.
ISBN 0-9627123-6-1

THE HARVEST

A "SCIENCE/POLITICO" NOVEL

From today's headlines predicting human cloning comes the emergence of "vaccos"—living "corporate cadavers"—raised to be sources of human organ and tissue transplants. One exceptional vacco will escape. His survival will depend upon Chris Turner, a sexual renegade who will love him and kill to keep him alive.

"One of the Ten Best Books of 1997," **Lavender Magazine**, Minneapolis. "In George Nader's *Chrome*, the hero dared to fall in love with a robot. In *The Harvest*—*a vastly superior novel*, Chris Turner falls in love with a vacco, Hart256043." Jesse Monteagudo, **The Weekly News**, Miami, Florida.

Finalist, 1997 Lambda Literary Award, Gay and Lesbian Science Fiction.

The Harvest. 216 pages. $11.95.
ISBN 0-9627123-7-X

THE LOVER OF MY SOUL

A SEARCH FOR ECSTASY AND WISDOM

Brass's first book of poetry since *Sex-charge* is worth the wait. Flagrantly erotic and just plain flagrant—with poems like "I Shoot the Sonovabitch Who Fires Me," "Sucking Dick Instead of Kissing," and the notorious "MTV Ab(*solutely*) Vac(*uous*) Awards," *The Lover of My Soul* again proves Brass's feeling that poetry must tell, astonish, and delight.

"An amazingly powerful book of poetry and prose," **The Loving Brotherhood,** Plainfield, NJ.

The Lover of My Soul. 100 pages. $8.95.
ISBN 0-9627123-8-8

How to survive your _own_ gay life

AN ADULT GUIDE TO LOVE, SEX, AND RELATIONSHIPS

The book for adult gay men. About sex and love, and coming out of repression; about surviving homophobic violence; about your place in a community, a relationship, and a culture. About the important psychic "gay work" and the gay tribe. About dealing with conflicts and crises, personal, professional, and financial. And, finally, about being more alive, happier, and stronger.

"This book packs a wallop of wisdom!"

Morris Kight, founder, Los Angeles Gay & Lesbian Services Center.

Finalist, 1999 Lambda Literary Award in Gay and Lesbian Religion and Spirituality.

How to Survive Your Own Gay Life. 224 pages. $11.95.
ISBN 0-9627123-9-6

ANGEL LUST

AN EROTIC NOVEL OF TIME TRAVEL

Tommy Angelo and Bert Knight are in a long-term relationship. *Very* long—close to a millennium. Tommy and Bert are angels, but different. No wings. Sexually free. Tommy was once Thomas Jebson, a teen serf in the violent England of William the Conqueror. One evening he met a handsome knight who promised to love him for all time. Their story introduces us to gay forest men, robber barons, castles, and deep woodlands. Also, to a modern sexual underground where "gay" and "straight" mean little. To Brooklyn factory men. Street machos. New York real estate sharks. And the kind of lush erotic encounters for which Perry Brass is famous. Finalist, 2000 Lambda Literary Award, Gay and Lesbian Science Fiction.

"Brass's ability to go from seedy gay bars in New York to 11th century castles is a testament to his skill as a writer." *Gay & Lesbian Review*.

Angel Lust. 224 pages. $12.95.
ISBN 1-892149-00-1

Warlock

A NOVEL OF POSSESSION

Allen Barrow, a shy bank clerk, dresses out of discount stores and has a small penis that embarrasses him. One night at a bathhouse he meets Destry Powars—commanding, vulgar, seductive, successful—who pulls Allen into his orbit and won't let go. Destry lives in a closed moneyed world that Allen can only glimpse through the pages of tabloids. From generations of drifters, Powars has been chosen to learn a secret language based on force, deception, and nerve. But *who* chose him—and what does he really want from Allen? What *are* Mr. Powars's dark powers? These are the mysteries that Allen will uncover in *Warlock*, a novel that is as paralyzing in its suspense as it is voluptuously erotic.

Warlock. 226 pages. $12.95.
ISBN 1-892149-03-6

the Substance of God

A SPIRITUAL THRILLER

What would you do with the Substance of God, a self-regenerating material originating from Creation? The Substance can bring the dead back to life, but has a "mind" of its own. Dr. Leonard Miller, a gay bio-researcher secretly addicted to "kinky" sex, learned this after he was found mysteriously murdered in his laboratory while working alone on the Substance. Once brought back to life, Miller must find out who infiltrated his lab to kill him, how long will he have to live—and, *exactly*, where does life end and any Hereafter begin?

Miller's story takes him from the underground sex scenes of New York to the all-male baths of Istanbul. It will deal with the longing for God in a techno-driven world; with the persistent attractions of religious fundamentalism; and with the fundamentals of "outsider" sexuality as both spiritual ritual and cosmic release. And Miller, the unbelieving scientist, will be driven himself to ask one more question: Is our often-censored urge toward sex and our great, undeniable urge toward a union with God . . . the *same* urge?

"Perry Brass has added to the annals of gay lit." ***Book Marks***.

The Substance of God. 232 pages. $13.95.
ISBN: 1-892149-04-4

The Manly Art of Seduction

HOW TO MEET, TALK TO,
AND BECOME INTIMATE WITH ANYONE

Winner Gold Medal Ippy Award from Independent Publisher,
Gay and Lesbian Non-Fiction

"Men are not supposed to be seductive." Perry Brass proves this is not true. Always waiting for someone else to make the first move, traumatized by your fear of rejection and don't have a clue how to open a conversation or expand the terms of a relationship, then *The Manly Art of Seduction* is a must-have. Brass explains male territorialism, and how it keeps men locked inside themselves. He talks about making decisions yourself, and how these decisions can be used to make seduction possible—even easy. He deals with rejection, and how to use mind pictures and exercises to rejection-proof your psyche. At the end of chapters are questions you can use to tailor this book to your needs, seeing your own progress as you come to master this art.

"A first-class primer for every taste,"

Richard Labonte, **BookMarks**, nationally
syndicated column about glbt books.

"Filled with useful, practical advice, Brass also explores deeper concepts like valor and territorialism, and his stunning chapter on rejection should be a must-read for everyone in the dating scene."

Elizabeth Millard, **ForeWord Reviews**, January, 2010.

"What Brass does so well is guide a man in how to get from the initial meeting all the way to the first date and beyond. But the brilliance of the book is that you can actually read it from the perspective of the person being seduced. The "seductee" can see just how open and vulnerable the person approaching them is being, and also see what types of responses they might end up getting back. The seductee might then see himself and begin to understand how his behavior might be affecting the situation. And in that, he might learn how to let down his own guard, and allow that connection to take place."

Kevin Taft, **Edge Magazine: Boston**. March 1, 2010

The Manly Art of Seduction, 200 pages, $16.95.
ISBN: 978-1-892149-06-0
Ebook ISBN: 978-1-892149-10-7

King of Angels

A NOVEL ABOUT THE GENESIS OF IDENTITY AND BELIEF

Set in the haunting, enchanting landscape of Savannah, Georgia (*Midnight in the Garden of Good and Evil*), during the tumultuous early 1960s (the *Mad Men* era), *King of Angels* differs greatly from most novels with an lgbt theme: it is about a significant and extremely compelling relationship between a father and son—told from the bond that both father and son feel, despite differences in generation, the many secrets that separate them, and barriers of temperament but not of basic character. This nourishing father-and-son relationship is something many gay men (as well as straight men) seek, but it has been sadly missing, and missed, from most literature.

King of Angels explores this bond as part of a re-examination of the male gender and role. As Benjamin Rothberg, the half-Jewish, 12-year-old protagonist of *King of Angels* says about Robby Rothberg, his very tragic but heroic Jewish father, he was the "closest thing to a brother I'd ever have, even though I didn't know it then."

Finalist, Ferro-Grumley Award for Gay and Lesbian Fiction, winner Bronze Medal IPPY Award for Best Young Adult Fiction. 2012.

King of Angels, 370 pages, $18.00.

ISBN: 978-1-892149-14-5

Carnal Sacraments

A HISTORICAL NOVEL OF THE FUTURE,
SET IN THE LAST QUARTER OF THE TWENTY-FIRST CENTURY,
2nd EDITION.

A white-knuckle suspense story set in the year 2075, the distant yet close-enough future, when constant corporate + government surveillance is Standard Operating Procedure. Endless war and endless "security" punch their way through individual lives. And your job level will determine exactly *if* and *how* you live and *die*. In a glittering city in a very internationalized Germany, Jeffrey Cooper, Alabama-born design star, has made a pact with the Devil himself. No matter what age he is, the mega-Corporation running the world will keep him looking movie-star young and handsome. Cooper has left his past, his history and heart behind. But they will catch up with him when he meets a handsome young Dutchman who offers him his real soul back—but with an even higher price than the Corporation is making him pay.

A perfect tale for the age of Edward Snowden, the National Security Agency, and a world business culture in which many gay men have taken key roles and given up so much of themselves in return. *Carnal Sacraments* is a book you won't put down until the very end.

"The most unusual novel I've read in years,"

Bay Area Reporter, San Francisco.

This new edition has a Foreword by the author, and an arresting new cover featuring a painting by Symbolist German artist Sasha Schneider.

Carnal Sacraments, 316 pages, $17.95.

ISBN: 978-1-892149-18-3

At Your Bookstore, or from:

Belhue Press
2501 Palisade Avenue, Suite A1
Bronx, NY 10463

E-mail: belhuepress@earthlink.net
Please add $3.50 shipping for the first book and $1.00 for each book thereafter. New York State residents please add 8.25% sales tax. Foreign orders in U.S. currency only.
You can now order Perry Brass's exciting books online at www.perrybrass.com.
Please visit this website for more details, regular updates, and news of future events and books.

Notes for Yourself

Please feel free to jot down ideas and questions for yourself inspired by *The Manly Pursuit of Desire and Love.* You can also friend Perry Brass on Facebook (https://www.facebook.com/perry.brass), keep up with him on Huffington Post (http://www.huffingtonpost.com/perry-brass/), and on Twitter (http://twitter.com/perrybrass). For more information about Perry and his work: http://www.perrybrass.com

CPSIA information can be obtained
at www.ICGtesting.com
Printed in the USA
FSOW02n1012110217
30711FS